LIVING IN SAN MIGUEL

JANE McCARTHY

© Copyright Jane McCarthy, 2005

ISBN # 0-9765805-1-9

Publicaciones Papelandia
Apdo 556, (www.mexicocolonial.com)
San Miguel de Allende, 37700 Gto., Mexico

TABLE OF CONTENTS

Preface
Take it Easy – Get on Mexican Time   1
Deciding to Live in San Miguel   5
    Should I Keep My House in the States?
    What Does It Cost to Live?
    What Will I Do?
    What's It Like Being a Single Woman Here?

Preparing for the Move   11
    Packing and Shipping
    Transshipping More Than A Few Boxes

Automobiles   15
    Accidents
    Bringing a Car from the States
    Buying a Car in Mexico
    Car Registrations
    Drivers' Licenses
    Gasoline
    Insurance
    Mechanics and Service
    Parking
    Rental Cars
    Tires

Banking   21
Basic Services – Utilities and Garbage   25
Bookstores and Greeting Cards   27
Bridge and Backgammon   29
Classes   31
    Acting
    Art
    Cooking
    Music and Dance
    Photography
    Writing

Colonias, the Neighborhoods of San Miguel   39
Communications Options Here and Abroad   47
    Receiving and Sending Mail
    Local Telephones
    Long Distance

    Television Hookups
    Satellite Connections
    Internet and E-mail Connections
Computers   55
    Consultants and Repairs
    Instruction
    Internet Cafes
EMERGENCY NUMBERS   59
Food and Water   61
    Bakeries
    Groceries
    Washing Fruits and Vegetables
    Water, Bottled
    Water Purification
    Water Testing
    Water Conservation
Gardening and Garden Design   65
Gay Life   67
Government Services and Police   69
    Identification cards
    Police and Security
    Domestic Violence
Guests – Where to Stay   71
Heating and Firewood   73
Hiring Household Help   75
    Maids
    Electricians, Plumbers and Handymen
Home Furnishings   77
    Appliances
    Ceramic Tile
    Fabrics
    Furniture
    Furniture, Outdoor
    Glass Table Tops
    Housewares and Decorative Items
    Interior Design
    Lighting Fixtures and Ceiling Fans
    Seamstress
    Upholstery and Slip Covers
Immigration   83
    The FM-T
    The FM-3

  The FM-2
  Can I Earn Money?
Kids' World   87
  Schools, Public and Private
  Kids' Activities
Laundries and Dry Cleaners   95
Measurement Conversions   97
Medical Services   99
  Medivac
  Hospitals
  Medical Doctors
  Dentists
  Drugstores
  Eye Glasses and Repairs
  Health Insurance
  Hearing Aids/Audiology
  Homeopaths, Acupuncturists and Reflexology
Medical Support Systems   107
  Home Health Care
  Medical Equipment
  Medical Alert System
  Making Final Arrangements
Night Life and Entertainment   109
Office Supplies, Business Cards   113
Personal Care   115
  Spas
  Massage
  Hairstyling
Pets in San Miguel   119
  Veterinarians
  Kennels and Grooming
  Dog and Puppy Training
  Adoption
  Bringing Down Your Horse
  Horseback Riding
  Horses – Boarding
Physical Fitness   123
  Yoga/Meditation
  Pilates
  Exercise
Real Estate   127
  Should I Buy or Rent?

　　　　Rent Now, Perhaps Buy Later
　　　　Can I Afford to Buy?
　　　　Buying Property
　　　　　　　Draw a Mexican Will
　　　　　　　Real Estate Lawyers
　　　　　　　Home Insurance
　　　　Construction and Renovation
　　　　　　　Building Permits
　　　　　　　Architects and Contractors
　　　　　　　Useful Books
　　　　Property Managers
　　　　Renting Your Home to Vacationers
Restaurants and Catering　　　　　　　　　　　　143
Service Clubs and Support Groups　　　　　　　147
Spanish – Learn It　　　　　　　　　　　　　　149
Sports　　　　　　　　　　　　　　　　　　　151
　　　Golf
　　　Tennis
　　　Bird Watching
　　　Sports Equipment and Rentals
Tax Preparation　　　　　　　　　　　　　　　153
Transportation and Tours　　　　　　　　　　　155
　　　　Airport Connections
　　　　Local Public Transportation
　　　　Buses to Points Outside San Miguel
　　　　Travel Agencies
　　　　Tours – Local and Out of Town
Volunteer and Donation Opportunities　　　　　161
Web sites and Books about San Miguel　　　　　165
Acknowledgements　　　　　　　　　　　　　167
Index　　　　　　　　　　　　　　　　　　　169

LIVING IN SAN MIGUEL

Preface

Living in San Miguel is for new residents who seek guidance on the practical side of starting their lives here and for visitors who are considering a move. It may also have curiosity value for voyeurs who simply want to know what it's like living here.

It may seem a bit nervy for a newcomer to write a book on San Miguel. But I'm experiencing on a daily basis the challenges of starting a new life. When I arrived the tank of gas for my apartment was empty. I had no hot water and didn't know why or what to do about it. I didn't know about utility bills being slipped under the door, the options for cable communications or the process for washing fresh vegetables. What newcomer is alert to the distinctive sound of clanging iron that signals the approach of the garbage truck?

As a recent newcomer I was struck by the lack of available basic information on how to start my life, such as options in cable and phone service, how to get the internet up and running, hire a maid, visa requirements, pay local bills, get pillows made and buy patio furniture, to name just a few.

My queries led me to believe that hundreds of other new households face the same challenges. So, why not make starting a new life here a bit easier with a guide that answers questions and suggests resources?

Even long-time residents should find this guide helpful. For example, when I wanted to know where to get ink cartridges for my copier, it took a number of inquiries before I was directed to a local source. That store was out of inventory and referred me to a store around the corner that nobody had mentioned. That source, and dozens more, are in the Guide.

San Miguel is growing rapidly. Well known as a destination for vacationers, it has become an alternative to retirement villages in Florida and New Mexico. Living here is less expensive and the cultural life is at least as active, if perhaps not as glamorous, as that in West Palm and Santa Fe. As the baby boomers reach retirement age and seek a much more active life than their predecessors, San Miguel is an adventurous alternative.

The currently accepted estimate is that 7,000 foreigners make their homes here. But a casual look at the large number of renovations and restorations underway suggests that this number is mushrooming.

Aside from new foreign residents flocking in from the States and Canada, San Miguel is now a favorite retreat for wealthy Mexico City residents who have million dollar homes on the hillsides overlooking San Miguel. In New York parlance, it's becoming the Hamptons of Mexico.

Growth may be spurred in part by the new 18-hole, Jack Nicholas-designed championship golf course, and the prospect of an international airport that would make San Miguel more accessible. The weak dollar and the high cost of establishing a nest in Italy or France are further incentives for Americans to look southward for their foreign adventure.

The *Living in San Miguel* guide seeks to fill a gap, suggesting resources that will help new residents adapt quickly and surely to their new setting and to feel at home. For vacationers who are considering, but are not yet committed to San Miguel, the guide should help them decide whether to pull up stakes and make a piece of San Miguel their own. As a newcomer advocate I admit that I'm not neutral in this regard.

The services listed are by and large recommendations from residents who responded to my many queries. As with any guide, listings are outdated even as the book goes to press. Every attempt has been made to be accurate, but errors inevitably occur. Perhaps subsequent editions will correct them and add services and opportunities as they arise. San Miguel, as we all know, is a vibrant and ever-changing town. That's why we're here.

Bienvenidos!

Jane Mc Carthy
March 2005

TAKE IT EASY - GET ON MEXICAN TIME

Even casual visitors to San Miguel comment on the town's languorous pace and relaxed rhythms. Businesses not related to tourists and dining take two-hour breaks between 2:00 p.m. and 4:00 p.m. Workers join their families for the mid-day meal. Taxi drivers and moms rushing home in their SUVs generally take the traffic in stride. It's only the anxious, impatient, high-strung Yankees who can't shrug off delays and interruptions.

Take the Time to Change Your Attitude

Chances are you were attracted to San Miguel in part for its slow moving, carefree ways. You, too, want a less hectic life. So, as a new arrival, try to get into the spirit of the town's soft and casual attitudes. Yes, you have dozens of errands to do to get your home up and running, but that doesn't mean everything needs to be done right now. Take the time to change your attitude. Adopt the San Miguel frame of mind. This may be difficult at first, but with every new challenge – waiting to be connected to the Internet, trying to find who delivers your gas – chant the mantra, *no es importante!* Leave your Type A personality in the States. It does no good here and will only increase your frustration. Deep breathing helps until you've mastered the new you.

A case in point is a friend who arrived in San Miguel in the late evening and promptly fell asleep, exhausted, in the house he had rented for an extended stay. In

Living in San Miguel

the morning he awoke early to find there was no electricity, no hot water and the telephone was dead. He sat on the edge of his bed, enraged. Then he saw a note from his landlady suggesting that if he had problems he should call a neighbor. He rang the neighbor's bell. She answered in her bathrobe, all smiles. Gritting his teeth he spouted, "I have NO hot water, NO electricity, NO telephone." In the few moments that the neighbor stood at her front door, the lights went on in his house. The power outage was over. "Well, one of your problems is solved," she cheerfully exclaimed. She then invited him in to take a shower and provided a towel. Later in the day the gas man came to light the boiler. Telephone service was more problematic. The landlady hadn't paid her bill. That took longer to straighten out - several weeks in fact.

Just Take it Easy and Say - Hey, This is Mexico

The lesson that all long-time residents learned years ago is that getting into a rage doesn't help. Neighbors and friends are accommodating and willing to help you out. Just take it easy and say - Hey, this is Mexico.

And in Mexico, manners are very important. In every transaction, *por favor* is an essential interjection. It's a simple, easy-to-give courtesy, a sign of respect that can make all the difference in your interactions. When you get into the swing of it you'll appreciate the value of such small niceties.

Try to be Calm, Controlled, and Most of all, Gracious

You may also have noticed that Mexicans never have tantrums on the street. It's really bad form to argue in public. They speak softly and don't raise their voices to their children. Perhaps their boisterous side is expressed in the incessant fireworks that boom with

Take it Easy

such regularity around every saints' day to ward off evil spirits. To fit in and enjoy the culture, try to be calm, controlled, and most of all, gracious.

The joy of San Miguel is that it IS different; it's not Houston. You have your reasons for being here. Remember that the first days are the most intense. Leaving family and friends is often difficult and you will probably wonder over and over if you were crazy to make the commitment. You'll know soon enough. In the meantime make a determined effort to appreciate your early days. If you let the Mexican way of living drive you up a wall you'll miss the great pleasures of smelling the pristine air, gasping at the beauty of a perfectly carved door, grinning at the uniformed tots on their way to school.

Don't Let the Business of Life Overtake You

In short, don't let the business of life overtake you. Give yourself the gift of being aware of the many wonders this new environment offers. San Miguel provides so many ways for you to reinvent yourself. There's a virtually unending parade of activities and a lively community that welcomes your participation. Volunteering service in dozens of causes that help needy Mexicans is an excellent way to find friends and satisfaction. Or develop a new avocation - printmaking, digital photography, horseback riding, acting or bridge. If you simply can't adapt but want to keep trying, San Miguel is loaded with therapists of every description. A casual reading of *Atencion San Miguel* can lead you to every specialty--New Age healers, astrologers, acupuncturists and certified psychotherapists.

You're in beautiful, wonderful Mexico, in a paradise that is San Miguel de Allende. Make it your own.

Living in San Miguel

DECIDING TO LIVE IN SAN MIGUEL

Is San Miguel the right place for you? As a visitor, you trek the cobblestones, gape at the glorious deep-blue skies, drink sunset margaritas on rooftop patios, and scan the enticing photos of homes for rent and for sale in real estate office windows. It's amazing to consider that in such a small community there are 16 recognized real estate firms, all eager for your business. Photos of gracious courtyards, living rooms with *boveda* ceilings, and rooftops with bougainvillea cascading down stucco walls are totally seductive. More than one casual tourist has said, "Let's just take a look." – and ends up buying the perfect *casita* on Hospicio.

Most potential residents have a number of personal, psychological and financial hurdles to overcome before they can make their homes here. No matter the beauty, the relaxed living and the attractions of being in a foreign yet friendly country, it's difficult to leave family and friends behind. Yes, modern technology makes it a snap to stay in touch, but you'll not be with your loved ones on their birthdays, be able to baby sit a grandchild in a pinch, or enjoy your usual entertainments with good friends you've known for years.

To make a successful life here you must be psychologically prepared to enter the Mexican culture in an open, accepting, non-judgmental way. If you constantly compare life in San Miguel to your life in Dallas, the move will be more difficult. You will make new friends, but it takes time. Are you psychologically ready to let yourself be in limbo for awhile? Are you

Living in San Miguel

willing to try out the yoga classes, hobbies and volunteer assignments that will help you make friends along the way? If you're married, is your spouse as enthusiastic as you are? The move could be a drag if your spouse is homesick and full of regrets. Perhaps a husband will miss the respect he gets from his friends for his past business or professional accomplishments. Or, a wife will be heart-broken to be torn from her grandchildren. In San Miguel the emphasis is on the here and now; your activities and enthusiasm here, not on what a big fish you were in your hometown. In this respect it's rather like going away to college; the equivalent of "what's your major" is the first question.

Another hurdle is the possible negative reactions from a few family members or friends. A good friend may opine that you're being selfish. How dare you just up and leave – it's unfair and disloyal. Yes, it is selfish. You are seeking an adventure, one that you hope will give you a better life.

If finances are a consideration, the decision takes on greater importance. There are no easy solutions. Take a hard-headed look at your finances and how they will work in San Miguel. This is an essential component in making the decision.

Should I Keep My Home in the States?

You may be in a financial position to straddle the fence; keep your home in the states and establish a new life here. This is ideal for married couples if one is hesitant. If you're unsure about whether you can leave your grandchildren and your friends behind, you should, if it's financially possible, keep your home. You can always rent it for awhile until you learn more. In many cases the rent from your home can go a long way to financing your life in San Miguel.

Deciding to Live in San Miguel

Other factors are taxes and capital gains. A tax consultant can help you with the finances. But the basic consideration is... Do you want to pull up stakes and establish a new life? If you know you want to do it, the technicalities are just that. If you're uncertain, don't burn your bridges.

What Does It Cost to Live Here?

Many newspaper articles assert that a couple can live in San Miguel on US$650 a month. For most of us this would be a stretch. You can save money by moving a distance away from Centro, but you'll probably need a car. The trek into town by public bus is a bargain ($4 pesos) but bags of groceries and other bulky items are awkward on a crowded bus.

Real estate agents estimate that the cost for a single person to live in San Miguel is around US$1,200 a month, plus the cost of renting or maintaining property. For a couple, the comparable cost would be US$1,600 a month. These figures include dining out frequently and occasional trips to other areas in Mexico.

Since a sizable chunk of the budget will go for rent, your living expenses will depend to a large extent on the size of your house or apartment and its proximity to Centro. As for groceries and household items, they are generally much less expensive than at home in the States. A New Yorker estimates that her housekeeping costs here are less than half of what they were in Manhattan.

Entertainment is a bargain. Many events charge no admission. Gallery openings with wine receptions are generally free. Tickets for the theater or lectures typically cost around $50 pesos.

In preparing the budget, don't forget to add in travel costs to the States if you have emotional commitments that will take you there once or more during the year.

Living in San Miguel

Also, decisions may need to be made about keeping U.S. Medicare health insurance.

What Will I Do?

Chances are you'll do a variation on what you did at home. If you volunteered for groups that helped troubled teenagers, you'll find a comparable group here. Bridge players have a built-in social network. If you are newly retired from a stressful job that you couldn't wait to leave, you'll probably enjoy the chance to relax and take the time to adapt to the new surroundings. In time, something surprising will grab you.

Almost everyone who comes here marvels at how busy she is. First it's getting your home in order and feeling comfortable. You'll meet people and a few of them will be your new pals. You'll find colleges, grandchildren, home towns and interests in common.

The one *caveat* is that residents here are less interested in who you were back home than they are about who you are now. This is a chance for reinvention and the exploration of new interests. "I'd always wanted to paint." You can certainly do that here. Meditation? Belly dancing? Horseback riding? All are available.

Many residents have to juggle their entertainment choices. Can I attend a flamenco concert featuring a world renowned guitar player at 5:00 p.m. and still go to the SMA Playreaders at St. Paul's at 7:30 p.m.? Does an intriguing movie at the Santa Ana Theater take precedence over a gallery opening? In San Miguel most events are within walking distance. If you go alone there's usually someone interesting to talk with.

Since you may be starting a new life, be sure it's the one you want to live. Consider how much time you want to spend alone, and how much is healthy for you. Perhaps you have solitary pursuits, such as meditation, drawing or writing. Figure out the time of day that's most productive for these ventures and leave space for them on a regular basis.

The "Wednesday Lunch Group," offers a perfect social opportunity. These friendly gatherings, held at different restaurants each week, provide instant contacts with other women and a chance to ask San Miguel veterans questions about coping in this new environment. The location of the lunches, which start at 2:00 p.m., is posted at **La Conexion,** Aldama #3.

What's It Like Being a Single Woman?

Every single woman will tell you, "don't expect to find a man in San Miguel." The well-worn adage goes, "All the men in San Miguel are married, gay or leaving on Tuesday." Most of the active, sexy, "with it" women go on at length about the lack of engaging men. Well, that's true all over America! After a "certain age" the pool of "available" men seems to dry up. Don't come here to find a man, or anywhere else for that matter. San Miguel has a large network of active women pursuing their own interests and profit-making ventures. They are generous and welcoming. Take full advantage of them.

With the well-publicized, if perhaps inaccurate, estimate that women outnumber men in San Miguel by 6 to 1, it's a wonder that so many single women continue to come here. Can it be that they feel comfortable? Yes, it's generally safe here, with the usual precautions. Women feel free to go out alone at night. Security may be a factor, but there's something else – the freedom to be yourself. Change your name, open a New Age spa? Why not? This may not be your cup of tea, but it won't take much time to find like-minded colleagues.

Living in San Miguel

The women in San Miguel are dynamos of entrepreneurship. They open shops, sell cosmetics, do acupuncture, read horoscopes, teach music, Pilates and yoga--and buy and renovate property.

Don't expect to find instant friends. Anywhere you go this takes some time and luck. But be assured you'll find compatible compatriots along the way. Take the time to breathe, soak up the views, find your interests -- and friendships will follow.

What's different here is that your acquaintances, neighbors and new friends have, by and large, left their friends and family behind. They are like-minded souls. They're not obsessing about their children and grandchildren; chances are there're here to escape these responsibilities. They want their own time; their own interests. This is your time to try out new avocations, consider satisfying volunteer opportunities, and expand intellectual horizons. If you do so, even in a limited way, the personal rewards will be surprising.

PREPARING FOR THE MOVE

So, you've made the decision to give yourself an adventure in San Miguel. Now what? Visions of your life here have been idyllic; now the down-to-earth challenges of the move seem formidable. The euphoria of signing the lease or purchase documents is replaced by more immediate concerns. Chances are you no longer travel with only a backpack. You want your creature comforts. Friends and family at home may be casting a skeptical eye. It's exciting to take the plunge but there are obstacles – practical, personal, and psychological. *Living in San Miguel* can help you with the practical—for everything else you're on your own.

If you've rented or purchased a home you will undoubtedly want to bring a few treasures to San Miguel. What to bring is among the first decisions. Of course family pictures, a few books and special items with sentimental value are a must. Most of your ordinary needs can be met here, but a few items are in short supply or of inferior quality. One of them is pens – everyone seems to be searching for a pen and locally-purchased pens don't work very well. Some other items that are generally unavailable or expensive are the latest computers and related gadgets, and battery chargers. For the kitchen, it's hard to find white balsamic vinegar, Celestial Seasonings tea, salad spinners, good kitchen knives, and cookware.

Many of the large U.S. stores have outlets in Queretero, only an hour's bus ride away, and in Leon, a longer trek. Mega stores such as CostCo, Home Depot, WalMart, Office Max, Office Depot and Sears, carry a full range of products. The CostCo in Celaya is closer

Living in San Miguel

than Queretaro and easier to find. However, the merchandise in these stores is aimed at the Mexican shopper and some products, such as sheets, towels and cookware, are not up to U.S. standards and prices are high.

To prepare for the move, it's obvious that you should clear up all your local bills and arrange to put as many of your regular payments (mortgages, home insurance, health care premiums) on automatic withdrawal from your bank account. Consider using automatic, electronic deposits for monthly Social Security checks and other regular monthly infusions from brokerage and trust accounts. To simplify your life, set up your bank accounts online so that you can pay bills, credit cards and examine bank balances and payments through the Internet.

If you use exotic prescription drugs, you should probably bring several months' supply. Commonly prescribed drugs are available here, over the counter, and at a substantial discount from U.S. prices. Stateside prescriptions for "controlled substances" are not valid here; a local doctor will need to write the prescriptions. If you are unsure about availability, arrange with an online pharmacy to handle your needs.

Packing and Shipping

If you are shipping only a few boxes of goods, not a household full of furniture and appliances, there are several shipping companies that are reliable and efficient: **La Conexion, Border Crossings** and **Solutions**. They suggest that you label the boxes "Used Clothing and Household Goods." The shipping fee is based on the size of the box and poundage. A typical box the size of a case of wine will cost between $25 and $40, depending on whether you've packed exercise weights or scarves. Of course, stateside shipping to the border town is extra. Your goods will come in by truck probably

Preparing for the Move

through Laredo, Texas. Delivery time is amazingly short, usually less than a month.

La Conexion. U.S. mailing address: 220 N. Zapata Hwy. #11, Laredo, TX 78043-4464. To set up an account locally, go to Aldama #3. By e-mail, click on www.aconex@prodigy.net.mx. **152-1599**, **152-1687**, and **152-6173**.

Border Crossings. U.S. mailing address: 413 Interamerica #1, BC-2323, Laredo, TX 78045-8285. To set up an account: Locally at Correo #19. by e-mail, click on pack@bordercrossingssma.com. **152-2497.**

> **Mark Bartell** is a highly reliable shipper for moving lots of boxes. A load of around 40 large boxes will cost around U.S. $2,000. He does not handle furniture or appliances. **152-8108.** bartell@cybermatsa.com.mx.

Solutions provides a U.S. mailing address and mailboxes for a minimum of 3-months rental for $60. To set up an account locally go to Recreo #11. By e-mail, click on sanmiguelsolutions@yahoo.com **152-6152.**

Transshipping More Than a Few Boxes

Be careful in selecting a mover for the Mexican part of the journey. There are a number of unscrupulous movers who'll quote low prices and will then hold your goods hostage until you pay them more money. It helps to get a quote in writing as a small gesture of good faith.

Transshipping a house full of goods is more complicated. To ship a houseful of furniture and appliances duty free requires an FM-3 visa for both you and your possessions. This is best arranged in the States. The international shipper you select will bring your goods to the border, probably to Laredo. They will then be

Living in San Miguel

transferred to a Mexican shipper who will complete the journey into Mexico.

A complete inventory of your goods must be compiled in Spanish. Major appliances, such as stoves, refrigerators, washers and dryers should top the list. Serial numbers must be provided. Newly purchased appliances should be taken from the boxes and lightly scuffed up to make them look used. Wash the inside of the refrigerator with detergent and keep the door open to remove the telltale scent of a new purchase.

Boxes of kitchen gadgets can simply be labeled *cocina*, and boxes of clothes tagged *ropa*. The total inventory must be given a value. The estimate should be on the low side, since if you want to ship your household goods back to the States the value at that time has to be at least the amount you claimed when the goods were brought down. The idea here is that the Mexican government doesn't want you to sell your U.S. goods here in Mexico.

This is just the basic information to get you started; there's lots of fine print. An advisor on Mexican law and immigration can help untangle the bureaucratic red tape.

Automobiles

AUTOMOBILES

One of the best things about San Miguel for many of us is that cars are not needed. Between buses and taxis you can go anywhere. But if you would be lost without wheels, be prepared for a challenge. Learn how to park with inches to spare between vehicles. In Centro, several long-term parking garages are available for about $50 a month, or you can look for a homeowner who doesn't use his garage.

ACCIDENTS

Horrendous stories are told about the trauma associated with even minor accidents, particularly if they involve a pedestrian. If there's any question of bodily injury the driver may be put into jail, a really unpleasant experience that can last overnight, with no food or warmth provided. If the accident occurs during business hours, however, you can post bail. And the car is impounded. Even if the pedestrian is given hospital X-rays and no injury is found, claims of injury can tie up the driver for months. If the driver wants to leave the country in the interim she must get special permission.

A Mexican insurance policy, however, brings an agent to your aid and is invaluable for cutting red tape.

These unfortunate experiences may be a result of not understanding the system. City officials say that an overnight stay in jail can be avoided if bail is paid and the driver is not intoxicated. An arrested person has a

Living in San Miguel

right to make a telephone call, have a translator present and a public defender. Bail is paid to the Ministerio Publico (District Attorney.) **154-9451** or **154-9452**.

Alberto is considered a professional for bodywork and painting. Drive through the green doors at Calzada de la Luz #67-A, near Pollo Feliz. The manager/owner is Raul.

Bringing a Car From the States

If you drive your car down from the States, you can expect two immigration stops. At the border your paperwork will be checked. Required papers include your passport, driver's license, proof of ownership or written permission from your financing company allowing you to cross the border, notarized proof of Mexican insurance and a valid major credit card. At the second stop, shortly after you've left the border, your car will be checked for contraband and you will be required to purchase an official car sticker.

Many residents suggest that border crossings can be expedited if an import permit is obtained before leaving the States. This can be done on the Internet at www.banjercito.com.mx. On the left side of the screen, click *Importacion Temporal de Vehiculos – Contatanos.* Or, call toll-free **1-866-356-0088**.

For a more detailed list of requirements for crossing the border check out www.portalsanmiguel.com. Click *Relocation* on the left of the screen.

Buying a Car in Mexico

New car purchases in Mexico cost about 20% more than comparable cars in the States, but there are advantages to buying locally. You will have a Mexican license plate and you can sell the car here. U.S. license plates cannot

Automobiles

be exchanged for Mexican plates, and U.S. cars brought from the States are not supposed to be sold in Mexico. If a car with U.S. plates is sold to a U.S. citizen, the car must be driven back to the U.S. and re-registered with the name of the new owner and then driven back to Mexico. The premium paid for a car purchased in Mexico can be recouped when the car is sold. The premium is mostly the result of high taxes.

Car Registrations

Some long-term residents keep their stateside license plates and let them expire. Since they have Mexican insurance, there seems to be no need for up-to-date registration. If they decide to take the car back to the States they reactivate the registration.

Drivers' Licenses

Many long-term residents need Mexican licenses because they can no longer renew licenses acquired in the States. The application requires copies of your passport, FM-3 or FM-2, and a copy of a bill sent to your San Miguel address. The written drivers test, in Spanish, has 30 questions. You are allowed to bring an interpreter for the test. The various requirements change periodically so it's best to inquire first and get the necessary forms together. Information is available at the **Transito** office (*Delegacion de Transito y Transporte*) at Correo #26, on the second floor, on the outdoor terrace.

When driving you are required to carry your FM-3 in the car. If you are stopped by the police you will probably be asked to produce it.

Gasoline

Gasoline is provided by PEMEX, the state-owned petroleum company. Prices are pegged to world oil prices. In October, 2004, the price of regular unleaded gas (Magna) was about U.S. $6.20 pesos per liter; Premium was U.S. $7.3 pesos per liter. This works out to about US$2.50 a gallon for regular unleaded gas.

Insurance

Mexpro (Mexico Insurance Professionals) sells auto insurance over the Internet. Prices are quoted for the coverage selected and the policy can be printed out directly from the computer. www.mexpro.com.

Point South RV Tours, in Moreno Valley, CA is highly recommended for car insurance in Mexico. Rates are considered very good and insurance can be obtained before leaving the States. Contact the agency's owner, Harlen Hudson. **1-800-421-1394.**

Lewis and Lewis, out of Beverly Hills, CA specializes in selling insurance for cars being driven in Mexico. Full coverage starts at about U.S. $260 a year. Online application is available. **1-800-966-6830.** www.mexicanautoinsurance.com

Deserve writes limited and full protection auto insurance. The company also offers temporary insurance for driving in the United States. Prices are considered to be very competitive. Posada de San Francisco, Plaza Principal #2. **152-5050.**

Lloyd's also sells car insurance. They will provide a rider to the Mexican policy that covers driving in the United States; however many residents say they've found better rates elsewhere. San Francisco #33. **152-4100.**

GEICO sells insurance for driving in the States. For prices check the Internet. www.geico.com

Automobiles

Mechanics and Servicing a Car

Ford and **General Motors** have dealerships for new and used cars and large repair shops. **Chrysler** sells new cars and has limited servicing.

English-Speaking Mechanics

Billy Sydney is highly recommended by car owners. He's on Prolongacion de Aldama. **152-4917.**

Julio Cesar Estrada is recommended as a car mechanic. **044-415-100-5913.**

Uribe is also considered extremely skilled. Col. Allende. **152-1974.**

Parking During the Day

New parking meters are being planned for the Centro in order to discourage long-term parking. The mayor estimates that the typical car parked in Centro stays in place for 13 hours. Parking will be limited to 2 hours in Centro; $10 pesos an hour. Stiff fines of up to US$100 will be imposed for violators.

The new meters will be attached to walls and placed to be as inconspicuous as possible. They will take pesos, paper money and credit cards. The meters are expected to generate around US$800,000 a year, which will be used for restoration projects within the historic district.

With the impending strict time limits on parking, many residents who work in town will have to use public parking lots during the day. The mayor is encouraging the construction of new lots around the perimeter of Centro to accommodate these vehicles. Currently there are two major lots in the downtown area.

Living in San Miguel

Mesones #46-B. Large lot: $12 pesos an hour; $50 pesos overnight, from 9:00 p.m.-9:00 a.m. Open from 7:30 a.m.-10:00 p.m.

Insurgentes #32. Stacked car parking. $15 pesos an hour; $52 pesos overnight, from 7:00 p.m.-10:00 a.m.

Rental Cars

Rent-a-Car agency rents small cars without air conditioning for between $612 pesos and $707 pesos a day, including unlimited mileage, taxes and insurance. Larger cars with air conditioning cost $985 pesos. Open 9:00 a.m.-2:00 p.m.; 4:00 p.m.-7:00 p.m. Located inside the Hotel Posada San Francisco, Plaza Principal, across from the Jardin. www.holarentacar.com. **152-0198.**

Tires

Cobblestone streets and rough terrain play havoc with tires and wheel alignments. Many residents suggest Michelin tires for their durability. Mexican tires are said to be longer lasting than their American counterparts.

Llantera Caracol, is a full-service garage that sells Goodyear tires. Open weekdays 9:00-5:00. Libramento El Caracol S/N, **(415) 152-2304** and **152-1983.**

LLycsa, sells Goodrich tires. Carretera a Celaya Km. 1, (415) **152-2325.**

Olimpia Zuniga does tire alignments and balancing. They sell Uniroyal and Michelin tires. Open weekdays 9:00 a.m.-6:00 p.m. Salida a Celaya #68. **152-4458.**

BANKING

In general, all banking transactions (except real estate purchases and rentals) are in pesos. Bills for gas, telephone, water, and cable are paid in pesos. While some new residents open peso bank accounts, many prefer to stay with dollars and use ATMs for their peso needs.

Mexican banks and Lloyd's pay substantially higher interest rate for accounts in pesos but it may be cumbersome and costly to reconvert to dollars if they are needed. BANORTE is the only bank that allows withdrawals in either pesos or dollars, with a Mexican bank card.

Lloyd's is considered to be particularly customer-friendly. For a fee, peso account customers can arrange for the bank to pay maids, gardeners and other help when you are out of town. The bank will also pay utilities, with the exception of cable bills.

Be watchful in exchanging dollars for pesos. The peso is a volatile currency that ranges widely. When buying pesos with dollars, check the exchange rate and bring dollars into Mexico when the peso is weak, that is, when you can get the most pesos for the dollar. Most residents draw dollars into their peso accounts only when pesos are needed in the near future. Exchange rates can be checked on the Internet at www.x-rates.com.

Getting cash at the ATM machines generally means being saddled with a wad of $500 peso notes that cannot

Living in San Miguel

easily be broken into smaller bills. Grocery stores (Gigante, Espino's and Bonanza), liquor stores, restaurants, bars and hotels usually have sufficient change to break large bills. Take every chance you get to use a large *peso* note. It's useful to keep a jar of change at home for occasions when you're out of small notes.

The listed Banks are popular with expats.

BANAMEX has a 24-hour ATM at Canal #4, across the street from the Jardin. Bank offices are open weekdays 9:00 a.m.-4:00 p.m.; Saturday, 10:00 a.m.-2:00 p.m. **152-1040** or **152-1004**.

BANCOMER SNC, Benito Juarez 11, **(415) 152- 0145**.

BANORTE has a 24-hour ATM at San Francisco #17. Many residents prefer this bank because cards for the ATM machines can be "swiped" through the machine so they can't be swallowed if there's a problem. Offices open weekdays 9:00 a.m.-5:00 p.m.; exchange hours are 9:00 a.m.-1:30 p.m. **152-0019, 152-7950** and **152-8099**.

BANCA SERFIN, San Francisco 32, **(414) 152-1161**.

LLOYD"S, at San Francisco #33, is open weekdays, 9:00 a.m.-5:00 p.m.; exchange hours 9:00 a.m.-3:00 p.m. The bank also offers car and medical insurance. **152-4100**.

Changing Money at Casas de Cambio

In Mexico, *Casas de Cambio*, or money changers, are not the seedy, hole-in-the-wall businesses found in much of the developing world. They are regulated and are a valid alternative to commercial banks. Many residents prefer *cambio* accounts because they are thought to have better rates of exchange and they

Banking

generally stay open longer hours. They handle wire transfers of dollars from the states and peso investments in interest-bearing securities and in Mexican stocks. Some will cash third-party checks.

Monex Open weekdays, 9:00 a.m.-3:00 p.m. Mesones #80. **154-4996.**

INTERCAM. To open an account you need to show title to property in Mexico and a copy of your passport and FM-3. Open weekdays, 9:00 a.m.- 6:00 p.m., Saturday, 9:00 a.m.-2:00 p.m. Correo #15, Juarez #27 and San Francisco #4. **154-6676, 154-6707** and **154-6660.**

Living in San Miguel

BASIC SERVICES

UTILITIES AND GARBAGE

New residents usually keep the name of the former owner, or a past, past owner on the utility bills. However, you may want to have your name on one of the utilities as proof of Mexican residency for DVD rentals and the like. A trip to the utility company with proof of residency and a small payment can effectuate the transfer.

Electricity

The bimonthly electricity bill will be slipped under your door. Take it seriously and don't forget to pay or your electricity will be cut off. Bills can be paid at local banks (for a service charge) or at the Farmapronto drugstores which stay open late and charge no fee. Farmapronto at Insurgentes #78 is conveniently located across the street from the Biblioteca. At the company offices at Loreto #13 there is usually a long line of bill payers. Payment windows open on weekdays, 8:00 a.m.-1:00 p.m. **152-0004.**

Electricity in Mexico is delivered at 110 volts, compatible for U.S. and Canadian appliances.

Gas

Beware the empty gas tank---you'll have cold showers and won't be able to boil water for morning coffee. Locate your gas tank and check the gauge to see how much is in the tank. If the arrow on the meter is in the

Living in San Miguel

red zone, call your supplier. Be prepared to pay in pesos, on the spot, including a modest tip. A typical tank holds 300 liters; the cost for filling the tank is about $1,200 pesos. Half a tank will generally last for about 2 months. Gas suppliers respond quickly, so you'll have gas within hours after a simple call, or often you can hail a gas truck as it goes by. Major suppliers are:

Gas Noel, 154-8383
Termo Gas, 152-2272
Gas Inem, 152-7777.

Water (SAPASMA)

Undoubtedly water will be flowing into your home. Water bills will be slipped under your door about every two months. The water company is not strict about payments; sometimes it lets a half-year go by without collecting and water will not be cut off without adequate notice. Water is inexpensive; for a small house the bill is about US$70 a year. Bills can be paid at local banks, or at the water office at Ancha de San Antonio #125, where payment can be made on weekdays from 8:30 a.m.-2:00 p.m. **152-4429** and **152-8155**.

Garbage Collection

A distinctive loud clanging of iron announces the approach of the garbage truck. It's on a more or less regular schedule, usually within an hour and a half range. In Centro, the trucks travel the north-south streets. Your neighbors will be on the corner with their plastic bags, waiting for the truck. It's a simple ritual that emphasizes for many gringos the amount of waste in our stateside "disposable" society. In Mexico there is substantially less garbage because there are fewer wrappings. Plastic bags are so valued that there's a charity in town that collects them to use as mattress filling for the needy. Garbage collection is a town service and provided without charge.

BOOKSTORES AND GREETING CARDS

Casa de Papel has a wonderful selection of high-quality greeting cards and journals. Also guide books, candles, note paper and gift items. Open during *siesta* hours. Mesones #57, inside the China Palace courtyard to the left. **154-5187.**

Libros el Tecolote probably has the largest stock of English language books in town, new and used; greeting cards and journals. The store is inside the courtyard of the Café Parroquia. Open Tuesday through Saturday, 10:00 a.m.-6:00 p.m.; Sunday, 10:00 a.m.-2:00 p.m. Jesus #11. **152-7395.**

El Colibri sells books, magazines and art supplies. Sollano #30. **152-0751.**

Biblioteca's Giftshop sells greeting cards and books about San Miguel. Hours are 10-7 Mon.- Fri., Sat 10-2 and Sunday before the "House and Garden Tour." Insurgentes 25. **152-7048.**

Living in San Miguel

BRIDGE AND BACKGAMMON

BRIDGE

Bridge is a major sport in San Miguel; games and lessons are offered at all levels. Generally the games are friendly and you'll be given a hearty welcome. It's a great way to meet people. Sunday seems to be the only day that bridge players take a break. The calendar is posted weekly in *Atencion*. Bridge players have several venues to choose from.

Duplicate Bridge Club at Stirling Dickinson #20; partner guaranteed. Sign in 15 minutes before play begins. **152-6298.**

The Bridge Studio at Santo Domingo #55, Interior 1; partner guaranteed. Play is low key, with lots of instruction for beginner and intermediate players. Duplicate games Wednesday and Saturday at 1:30 p.m. Lessons taught by Diamond Life Master Gary Mitchell and Gold Life Master Corinne Leachman. **152-6351.**

Villa Jacaranda has rubber bridge games on Friday at noon. Aldama #53. **152-0934.**

Bridge Lessons are also offered by
    Faye Guidry at **152-3426** and
    Fred House at **152-2406.**

Living in San Miguel

BACKGAMMON

Weekly games are held on Friday at 2:00 p.m. at the Café Santa Ana in the Biblioteca. It's a social game; bring your own set if possible.

CLASSES

Acting

Nancy Nugent is a drama coach who teaches acting and improvisation in both private and class settings. She does warmups for body and voice and uses theater games in her classes. Monologues are one of her specialties. laxmisma@yahoo.com. **152-6809.**

Art

Instituto Allende offers a comprehensive range of art courses, including stained glass, jewelry, batik and ceramics. www.instituto-alende.edu.mx. Ancha de San Antonio #20. **152-0190** and **152-0929**.

Centro Cultural Ignacio Ramirez has many art courses, including contemporary painting, figure drawing, sculpture, printmaking, textiles, stained glass and ceramics. Bellas Artes, H. Macias #75. **152-0289.**

Painting with Ink and Watercolors

Britt Zaist demonstrates the use of ink, acrylic and watercolor and discusses materials, techniques and composition. Students create their own artworks in 2-day workshops. Monday and Tuesday, 10:00 a.m.-2:00 p.m. Cost is $825 pesos, including materials. Estudio, Calle Atascadero, Callejon Sin Salida #14. www.artistsofsanmiguel.com/brittzaist. **152-6171.**

Living in San Miguel

Helen Coffee teaches watercolors on Friday from 10:00 a.m.-1:00 p.m. Bring watercolors, paper and brushes. Pre-registration required. $200 pesos. **152-1442.**

Drawing and Painting

Bonnie Griffith teaches "painting from the imagination." She uses abstract paintings, collage and mixed media to open students up to new materials. Her studio is in Centro. She takes one or two students at a time. **152-3024.**

Nina Wisniewski holds 2-session, 2-hour workshops that take students around San Miguel for their artistic endeavors. All levels of experience are welcome. Cost for drawing is $600 pesos; for painting, $800 pesos. Beneficencia #15. www.sanmiguelguide.com **044-415-15-12462.**

Keith Keller has two well-lighted studios where he teaches month-long classes for beginners and experienced painters. No pre-registration. Walk-ins are welcome. Classes on Monday, Wednesday and Friday Tuition is $1,980 pesos a month. Ancha San Antonio #27. www.sanmiguelartists.com/keithkeller. **152-0637.**

David Mallory gives 5-day workshops in Impressionist oil painting. Weekdays, 10:00 a.m.-noon and 2:00 p.m.-4:00 p.m. The cost is $1,400 pesos, including materials. His work can be seen at his studio at Zacateros #73. **154-8455.**

Charcoal and Pencil

Rebecca Peterson uses everyday objects to demonstrate the power of light and shadow, contour and curve, in 2-session, 3-hour workshops. Previous experience not needed. Cost is $600 pesos, including materials. Pre-registration required. **154-7010.**

Classes

Ceramics
Joan Elena Goldberg has a home studio where she teaches wheel-throwing and decorative techniques. Beginning and advanced students. 3 classes a week are recommended. Pre-registration required. joanelena@hotmail.com. San Antonio Abad #36. **152-3844.**

Printmaking
Rodriguez/Navarro has one-day, hands-on workshops, Monday through Saturday, 10:00 a.m.-4:00 p.m. rodrigueznavarro@terra.com.mx. **15-151-7219**.

Gary Burkowitz conducts 5-day series of classes from 11:00 a.m.-2:00 p.m., in workshops that use printing to express artistic visions. Pre-registration is required. $1,375 pesos, includes materials. Reloj #46. www.sanmiguelartists.com/garyberkowitz. **152-2816.**

Papier Mache
Lisa Simms conducts 2-day workshops for creating masks, puppets and sculpture on Monday and Wednesday from 2:00 p.m.-6:00 p.m. $660 pesos, including materials. Pre-registration required. **152-5152**.

Jewelry
Jose Mario Bustamante holds 2-hour workshops for designing custom-made bracelets, earrings and necklaces using a wide variety of stones. Monday to Saturday. Walk-ins are welcome. $80 pesos, plus materials. Codo #9. **152-6078.**

Cooking Classes

Kris Rudolph, owner of **El Buen Café.** Full dinner with margaritas, Thursdays, 4:00 p.m.-7:00 p.m. For reservations drop by the restaurant at Jesus #23, or call **152-5807**.

Living in San Miguel

Victoria Challancin conducts cooking classes in Spanish for household cooks and maids. In addition to cooking techniques she gives instruction on sanitary food handling and preparation. She also has cooking classes in English for residents and visitors. Her *Flavors of the Sun* classes focus on the cuisines in warm climates such as Mexico, North Africa, the Mediterranean, Thailand and India. Classes by appointment. www.flavorsofthesun@yahoo.com. **152-5912.**

Sazon has a spectacular kitchen and the classes are always filled with good cheer. Drop in for a look around and a class schedule. Correo #22. **154-7671.**

Chef Maria uses authentic Mexican recipes to teach Mexican techniques and the way ingredients are used. Classes held daily. www.cocimari.com. Calle de la Luz #12. **152-4376.**

Las Hadas Madrinas (fairy godmother's place.) **Patsy DuBois** conducts country cooking classes at a ranchero on the road to Dolores Hidalgo. **185-2151.**
cell: **044-415-153-5303.**

Music and Dance

Centro Cultural Ignacio Ramirez has teachers of piano, cello, violin and viola and courses in chorus and music theory. They also offer classes in dance and ballet. Bellas Artes. H. Macias #75. **152-0289.**

Guitar: David Bar-Chai All levels of expertise welcome. **154-9239.**

Belly dancing classes are held at the Recreo Center, Recreo #4, Tuesday and Saturday at 11:00 a.m. for beginners; Thursday at 11:00 a.m. for intermediates. $40 pesos per class. Walk-ins encouraged. **154-4165.**

Photography and Digital Camera Club

Jo Brenzo has been teaching photography in San Miguel for many years. She teaches basic photography in a 5 day workshop at Bellas Artes. Cost is US$100. To register, contact Bellas Artes at **152-0289.** Jo teaches a 2-class series on hand-coloring of black and white photographs and computer prints; a 2-class series on photo transfer and manipulation; and a series on using a digital camera. For more information see her Web site at www.acdphotocom.

She also teaches darkroom techniques in a 3-class series on weekends at Cinco de Mayo #10, Colonia Allende. $1,320 pesos, including materials. Contact Jo directly at **152-2816.**

Robert de Gast is a professional photographer and author of *The Doors of San Miguel.* He offers private lessons to help you improve your camera skills. **152-7396.**

Skidmore Smith specializes in black and white handmade photographs. He's in the old-fashioned mode of emulsions and the darkroom. He teaches at the Universidad de Leon and in San Miguel takes students around the town to shoot. **415-45724.**

Photoshop Techniques

Bill Lieberman teaches photoshop techniques in a 4-class series from 10:00 a.m. to 1:00 p.m., Monday through Thursday, at the Computer Center, Mesones #57. The cost is $975 pesos. Contact Jo Brenzo at **152-2816**, or Bill Lieberman at **442-293-0112.**

Gary Berkowitz also conducts 4-class photoshop workshops at the Computer Center, Mesones #57. **152-2816**, or **152-2483.**

Living in San Miguel

Jo Brenzo offers hand-on instruction on cropping, exposure and color control, and sharpening images. The 4-day sessions meet Monday through Thursday, 11:00 a.m.-2:00 p.m., with computer lab time on Tuesdays and Saturdays, 4:00 p.m.-7:00 p.m. Tuition of $975 pesos includes materials and lab time. Pre-registration required. Computer Center, Mesones #57. **152-286.**

Digital Camera Club meets to explore the many-faceted ways digital photography can be used within the context of art. Pictures are shown on a movie theater size screen. Meetings are on the second Thursday of the month. Call Bob Ellison at **152-1365.**

Writing

The recently-organized Authors' Sala offers wonderful opportunities for new and experienced writers to get together to discuss their works. Writers bring their works for discussion and critique.

The Sala also presents readings from the works of many of San Miguel's noted authors. The popular and enthusiastic meetings are held usually on the first Friday of the month, from 5:00 p.m.-7:00 p.m., with a wine reception following the readings. Suggested donation is $50 pesos. Posada San Francisco, across from the Jardin. To check on the current schedule of offerings go to www.sanmiguelauthors.com.

Eva Hunter has been conducting writing workshops in San Miguel for 10 years. She's a widely-published author who specializes in nonfiction. A popular series is her *Workshop for Pros*. Cost for a 2-week series is US$250. She also has 1-day workshops. Hospicio #14. www.writersworkshopsanmiguel.com. **154-7921.**

Memoirs
Sally Riewald offers guidance to writers who want to turn their personal stories into professional material. Two-session classes are held on Tuesday and Thursday

from 10:00 a.m.-1:00 p.m. Pre-registration required. Cost is $550 pesos. **154-9923.**

The Novel

Richard Crissman helps writers turn their story ideas into novels. He works with authors on story flow, plot lines and character development. Classes on a flexible schedule. $200 pesos an hour. **152-7327.** www.richardcrissman.com.

Living in San Miguel

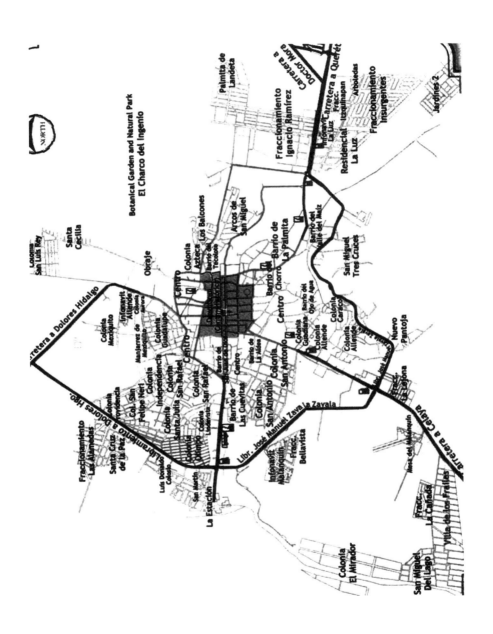

COLONIAS

The Neighborhoods of San Miguel

San Miguel spreads out in all directions from *El Centro*, into separate neighborhoods called *colonias*; smaller areas are called *barrios*. They are the old, traditional neighborhoods where many generations of families lived before the town's population expanded into the outskirts of San Miguel. There are 50 *colonias* and *barrios*. When exploring neighborhoods it helps to carry the large, glossy *Mapa* that roughly pinpoints the areas. It's available in bookstores and tourist shops. Maps of San Miguel don't tell the whole story since many neighborhoods are separated by deep gorges and ravines that don't show up on the map.

The close-in suburbs of San Miguel are defined on three sides by a perimeter highway called Libramiento a Dolores Hidalgo along the north and west perimeter; its name changes to Libramiento a Queretaro as it crosses the major intersection at the end of Salida a Celaya. The highway is on high ground overlooking the town and provides excellent vantage points to see the lay of the land.

As San Miguel continues to grow, many communities previously thought to be "out-of-town" are now "hot" development properties.

Living in San Miguel

CLOSE-IN COMMUNITIES

Southwest of Centro

San Antonio and Guadiana are *colonias* on either side of the Instituto Allende: Guadiana is just beyond the Instituto, on the same side of the street; San Antonio is a larger area directly across from the Instituto. The dividing line between them is Ancha de San Antonio. Both areas are popular with expats. It's an easy walk to Centro from these *colonias* and convenient for taking advantage of all the resources offered at the Instituto. Property is less expensive than in Centro, particularly in San Antonio. Guadiana has become extremely popular in recent years and property values reflect its popularity.

Caracol is a small neighborhood up the hill from Guadiana. Dirt roads are being paved with stones, giving the area a much more finished look. Many large homes are under construction. The steep hillsides afford excellent vistas.

Allende, just south of Guadiana, is becoming increasing popular. Foreigners, attracted by lower housing prices, have been moving into what was until recently a mostly Mexican community. The walk to town takes about 15 minutes along mostly level terrain. It's a picturesque area where construction and renovation are active.

Ojo de Agua is a *barrio* further south, abutting Callejon de Ojo de Agua. It has commanding views overlooking San Miguel. The area has large, expensive homes. A car is essential.

South of Centro
Chorro is a *barrio* with steep streets that overlook the Waterworks and Benito Juarez Park. It has large,

expensive homes and is a prime area for expats who have built spectacular homes.

Northeast of Centro
Azteca is a small area of steep streets that lead up from the Ignacio Ramirez covered market, off Homobono. At the top, the views of the gorges and ravines and an ancient aqueduct beyond are spectacular, particularly at sunset. The area is a mix of impressive homes and more modest dwellings. The hills are a challenge for any trekker.

Los Balcones, east of Azteca, is a high-priced area with large homes that have spectacular views of the town and the mountains beyond.

North of Centro
Obraje, north of Azteca, off the extension of Calzada de la Presa, has modest homes. The walk to town is manageable.

Guadalupe and **Aurora** are off Calzada de Aurora, on the left. They have the feel of traditional Mexican neighborhoods and are increasingly getting attention from foreigners who seek reasonably priced homes that are not too far from Centro.

East of Centro
Atascadero is an expensive area with large homes and expansive views of the rolling hillsides. It's a steep drive up Santo Domingo to the area around La Puertecita, the restaurant and hotel.

West of Centro
San Juan de Dios, is a *barrio* close to Centro, about a 10-minute walk. Its popularity has grown as foreign residents have come to appreciate the charm of the historic church and its spacious courtyard, and the steep streets that run off Beneficencia and the main artery, San Antonio Abad.

Living in San Miguel

San Rafael, across Avenida Guadalupe from San Juan de Dios, is considered to be the most dangerous area in San Miguel, although it varies from street to street. Some residents say they look out on the street to see if neighbors are walking about before venturing forth. This is reputed to be a territory for drug dealers; on some streets the night air is pierced with loud arguments and threatening behavior.

Independencia, north of San Rafael, runs along Avenida Independencia. The rather rundown look of the area is deceiving. Until recently it was a predominately Mexican community. Now, developers are building a wide cobblestone street with fancy lighting, up the Avenida and to the right. Expectations are that a luxurious gated community is in the offing. Still, large lots are available on the left side, overlooking all of San Miguel.

San Felipe is north of Independencia abutting the Libramiento. It's a predominately Mexican community with many vacant lots. But here too the construction scene is active.

Santa Julia, beyond Independencia, is another area where a few large homes sit comfortably with their smaller neighbors. Here, Mexicans and expats live a tranquil life. Less than a decade ago this was considered suburbia, but now most of the land has been taken. It's a short distance to town but still has the feel of the countryside. It would be difficult to live here without a car.

Olimpo is south of Santa Julia and, like Santa Julia, abuts the Libramiento. This is one of the last remaining areas where land is available. Olimpo originally was *ejido*, government land that was distributed in parcels to *campesinos*. The streets are laid out in a grid pattern. It's a mixed neighborhood that seems to lack financial strength, but it will probably not take long for it to catch up with other areas. The walk to town is about a half-hour.

Colonias

SUBURBAN COMMUNITIES

Southwest of Town
La Lejona is just beyond the Libramiento intersection with Salida a Celaya, in the south. It looks a bit seedy, with weed-filled vacant lots and many homes with for sale signs. Perhaps reflecting the rundown look of the neighborhood, homes are inexpensive. Three-bedroom homes can be purchased for around $100,000.

Malanquin is a small gated community with large lots surrounding the Malanquin Golf and Country Club, on the Road to Celaya, 3 kilometers from Centro. Homes are luxurious. It's populated mostly by foreigners and residents of Mexico City.

Los Frailes is beyond La Lejona, off Salida a Celaya, (the extension of Ancha San Antonio), after the intersection with the Libramiento. This large area has a distinctly suburban feel, with mixed neighborhoods that are predominately Mexican. It features beautiful views and well-tended small parks. The homeowners' association maintains the parks. Lots that could be purchased several years ago for around US$6,000 now cost between US$20,000 and US$25,000. It's becoming a hot spot for development and construction is in progress throughout the area.

Southeast
Residencial La Luz and **Izquinapan** are communities located in back of Gigante. They are predominately Mexican neighborhoods with modest homes. They are thought to be too far out of town to be desirable.

Ignacio Ramirez is a sprawling area of low-cost homes left of the main road, Blvd. de la Conspiracion, that runs in back of Gigante. It's a dilapidated, flat area, with the only attraction being a huge baseball field and soccer stadium.

Living in San Miguel

RURAL COMMUNITIES

San Miguel's rural communities extend as far as the green overhead sign that points the way to Dolores Hidalgo. The municipality of San Miguel is much like a county in the United States. It has the authority to give permits to dig wells and, in issuing building permits, considers whether there is nearby electricity.

Before signing a purchase contract for land in a rural area, look into the availability of utilities. San Miguel is no longer issuing permits to dig wells. The contract can contain a clause stating the utilities are available, but if this turns out not to be the case, you may lose the deposit if you decide to back out of the deal.

Off the Road to Dolores Hidalgo

Candelaria is a gated community that's close to town. Many expats have homes here and construction is ongoing.

Taboada, is another residential area. Electricity ends shortly after the turnoff so homes are equipped with solar power. Wonderful views of the lake. Homes with one or two hectares of land can be purchased for under US$200,000.

Los Charcos, just beyond the Taboada turnoff, is another area where homes have lots of land.

Parador de Cortijo is a mainly gringo community, off Dolores Hidalgo on the left. It's on the road to Atotonilco, about 7 miles from San Miguel. The enclave is quiet, but has the advantage of being close to the highway. Atotonilco is centered by an ancient church. It's a sleepy Mexican village with homes dotted over large plots of land.

Colonias

Las Labrodores is a new community with luxury homes under construction. The attraction here is its proximity to the planned Jack Nicholas championship golf course.

Off Calzada de la Estacion (the extension of Canal) **Tirado** is a horseback riding area that's close to town but rural in character. Small Mexican villages dot the area. Take Calzada de la Estacion to the end; turn left and go over the railroad tracks and turn right. The countryside is beautiful, with cultivated fields all around and mountains at the horizon.

La Cieneguita is further down the road. Many foreigners call this area home. It has a distinctly agricultural base. The small town square, off to the right, is charming.

Alternative Living
Permaculture Community is an international settlement that grows organic food, uses rain for its water supply and solar for power. There are presently nine homes; lots cost around US$8,000 for a hectare (2.5 acres.) It's about a half-hour from town, past Gigante on the road to Rodriquez, on Dr. Mora road, next to the village of San Jose de Gracia. For information, call Marcia Dunetz at **152-6191** or e-mail her at marciadunetz@prodigy.net.mex.

Living in San Miguel

COMMUNICATIONS OPTIONS HERE AND ABROAD

Receiving and Sending Mail

La Conexion and **Border Crossings** (and several others) have mailboxes for rent for a monthly fee of around US$20. Subscribing to this service will give you a U.S. address that friends, banks, credit card companies, magazines and other regular correspondents can use. The U.S. address is also helpful for ordering items on the Internet for purchases you want delivered here or shipments to friends in the United States.

These services will also send your mail, thus avoiding the vagaries of the Mexican postal service. For a small fee, about $5 pesos a letter, your mail will travel under the company's auspices to Laredo and be put into the U.S. postal system. U.S. postage stamps can be purchased from these shipping companies at their San Miguel locations. Subscribers can also use free Internet connections and make telephone calls to the States and Canada from their local offices.

Be sure to notify the U.S. Post Office of your change of address. Mail will be redirected to the new Laredo address for about 6 months. It's best to give at least two months' advance notice to important correspondents, such as banks, brokerage houses and credit card companies. Delivery of mail redirected by the post office can take a week or two.

Living in San Miguel

La Conexion. U.S. mailing address: 220 North Zapata Hwy, #11, Laredo, TX 78043-4464. Local address is Aldama #3. **152-1599, 152-1687** and **1526173**. www.aconex@prodigy,net.mx.

Border Crossings. U.S. mailing address: 413 Interamerica #1, BC-2323, Laredo, TX 78045-8285. Local address is Correo #19. pack@bordercrossingssma.com

Local Telephones
Land-line Telephones
If your home is equipped with a telephone, you're in luck. If not, and you want a land-line, call TELMEX. If you're fortunate a line will be available, but chances are you'll be told that the wait for service will run into several months. Unless you're patient and can wait for service you're only option is a cell phone.

The advantage of a TELMEX phone is that it can be dialed locally using a 7 digit number. Outside San Miguel, add the prefix 415.

Telephone numbers customarily stay with the house and the telephone is written into the sales contract. Initially, telephone numbers were given out sequentially. Thus the number 152-0012 would have been one of the earliest numbers.

TELMEX is widely criticized for unreliable service, particularly during the rainy season. One resident complained her service was on for only one week between May and October.

The complaint telephone number, **152-2331**, extension **050**, is answered electronically and is often unresponsive. If there's no response within 72 hours, customers are advised to call the number again. A visit to the TELMEX office only results in the service agent calling the 050 number once again. If service is

Communications

interrupted, TELMEX does not necessarily adjust the bill.

The monthly $180 peso charge for a telephone line includes 100 calls. Phone bills can be paid at the telegraph office, Correo #16, next to the post office, at TELMEX, or at banks. The Correo telegraph office is open weekdays 9:00 a.m.-3:00 p.m.; weekends, 9:00 a.m.-1:00 p.m.

TELMEX, Salida a Celaya #56. Open weekdays, 8:00 a.m.-2:00 p.m. **152-5222**, or **152-2331**.
    Repair service: 152-2331, extension 050.

Telephone Repairs
Daniel Guerray comes highly recommended. **154-6331** or **044-15-153-2583**.

Abraham Campos Ortega is also an expert in fixing telephones. **044-415-100-7718**.

Cell phones
Cells are widely in use and can be purchased at literally dozens of stores. **TelCel** is a popular outlet; phone purchase prices start below $600 pesos. There's no contract; the phone will belong to you. The cell is activated with phone cards that put minutes on the cell. A drawback of cell phones is that even for local calls, cell to cell, "044" must be dialed before the ten-digit number. Cell phone users calling a local land-line can use the 7-digit number.

Using your stateside cell phone in Mexico is costly. The beam goes to your home base to make a call in Mexico. If you treasure your U.S. telephone number, put your service on minimum usage (usually around US$20) before you leave.

Living in San Miguel

Long Distance
Through the Internet
For those with cable connections, long distance service is available via high-speed Internet using an assigned U.S. area code. If you opt for a Detroit area code, all calls that your Detroit friends make to you will be billed as local calls; your calls to them will be covered by a monthly service charge.

Vonage is the service many San Miguel residents use for long distance connections. It is a do-it-yourself installation. The company provides hi-speed Internet telephone and cable broadband with unlimited local and long distance service for a monthly charge of US$30, or US$15 for 500 minutes. To find out more, or to enroll in this service, click on www.vonage.com.

Packet8 is another long distance cable option that runs through the Internet. If you are cable savvy, you can probably install the connection on your own. Depending on the equipment you need, the cost to get it up and running is around US$300. You will have a U.S. area code of your choice. Monthly charges for unlimited calls are US$50. www.packet8.net. If you have problems with Packet8, call **408-654-0880** and ask for **Tyson**.

Skype is a free service for calling long distance anywhere in the world through the computer. Many residents recommend the service. All that's needed is a US$15 microphone that plugs into the computer. Or, you can plug in a more expensive headset. Some users say the service works better on Windows XP than on Windows 98. For more information see www.skype.com.

Direct Dial Long Distance
TELMEX charges $1.48 pesos a minute for calls within Mexico; calls to the U.S. and Canada are $4.57 pesos a minute.

Multicom offers access through an 800 number for international calls: Direct Dial to the U.S. and Canada

Communications

is US$0.20 per minute: Digital service is offered from US$0.09. No contracts or monthly payments. Correo #3. Multicom000@yahoo.com. **152-1579** and **152-6368**.

Cell Long Distance

Verizon, offers a North American plan that allows subscribers to use their stateside cell phones for inexpensive international calls. This option works well in San Miguel but not necessarily in other parts of Mexico. The cost is US$70 a month for 400 minutes during the weekday, plus 1,000 minutes for evenings and weekends.

Television Hook-ups

Cable TV Service

Tele Cable is the most popular cable company. If you have a cable connection in a rented home you will most likely be responsible for paying the bill. To pay the bill or make programming alterations you must go in person. Service is efficient but be prepared to wait for an English-speaking agent. Contracts are in the name of the owner, or previous owner of the property; for simplicity it is suggested that the name stay on the bill.

The basic contract that has Spanish language TV stations costs around $245 pesos a month including the required decoder. Add-on packages are available. U.S. channels range from a monthly cost of $22 pesos (BBC) to $153 pesos (Disney, HBO, Cinemax.) Monthly cable TV service with modest add-ons is around $300 pesos.

Installers come to your home in pairs to make the necessary adjustments. They are friendly, accommodating and diligent in making sure you understand the system. But they come unexpectedly. Just hope you're home.

Living in San Miguel

A little known fact is that to cancel your contract you must bring the cable box back to Tele Cable between the 1st and the 5th of the month.

Tele Cable, Salida A Celaya #95.
152-1942, or **152-3442**.

Satellite Connections

Sky and **DISH Network** are the two largest companies offering satellite connections in San Miguel. Sky recently purchased all the Mexican accounts of Direct TV. DISH is supposed to have the largest number of channels that come in clearly. For information about equipment, installation and services look at their Web sites: www.sky.com and www.dishnetwork.com.

Daniel Guerra is considered to be the local "pro" on satellite connections. He can be contacted at **154-6331** or **044-415-2583**.

Sonke Stuck is another recommended installer of satellite service. **01-461-117-1313**.

Internet and E-mail Connections

Cable

To receive e-mail at home through your computer and be connected to the Internet you'll need an additional service that Tele Cable provides. Depending on the speed of access to the Internet you require, the cost per month ranges from $219 pesos for 64 Kbps, to $677 pesos for 512 Kbps. Purchase of a cable modem is a one-time fee of $1,500 pesos (or $1,600 pesos for wireless.) Installation is $150 pesos.

The total monthly cost of an Internet connection at 256 Kbps is around $400 pesos per month. Contracts are billed forward and must be paid in person in pesos; you can save time and aggravation by paying several months in advance. Be sure to keep track of payment dates or your service will be cut off.

Tele Cable Salida a Celaya #95.
152-1942, or **152-3442**.

Dial-up

TELMEX provides dial-up Internet access. Of course you must have a telephone line. The cost for this service is $189 pesos a month.

TELMEX, Salida a Celaya #56. Open weekdays, 8:00 a.m.-2:00 p.m. **152-5222**, or **152-2331**.

Unisono net has dial-up access, including AOL access for e-mail. They provide do-it-your-self installation. Bilingual support service is available. . www.unisono.net.mx. H. Macias #72-B. **152-4958** and **152-6331**.

Living in San Miguel

COMPUTERS

New computers brought into Mexico are subject to a 17% tax. Used laptops can be brought in legally with no tax.

Consultants and Repairs

Sue Bolli is a computer specialist who knows hardware, software and wiring and she's a troubleshooter. She taught computer classes in Canada for 10 years. In San Miguel, she goes to residents' homes to teach them what they want to learn about their computers. Suebolli55@yahoo.com. Relox #58, Int. 3.
044-415-103-1657.

Daniel Guerra is recommended for all sorts of electronic repairs, including repairs on phones after outages, computers, satellites and audio/video equipment. He's considered a "treasure" with reasonable prices and a professional manner. His English is good. Daniel@intersystemas.com
154-6331 or **044-415-153-2583.**

Martha Lieberman is highly recommended for Macs. She's a specialist in problem solving and systems analysis. She is also a professional trainer on Mac equipment. mlresources@mac.com **152-1825.**

Herberto Guerera has been trained by Apple for computer repairs. He comes immediately and is very knowledgeable. **152-8618** and **152-8619.**

Living in San Miguel

Jason Tudisco is a computer programmer who creates Web pages and teaches people how to use their computers. He also helps with DVD hookups, Vonage and similar services. **152-7130** or **044-415-101-2671.**

Larry Gassler has years of stateside experience and has been in business in San Miguel for 9 years. He offers help with hardware and software programming, viruses and Trojan removal. E-mail at larsma@prodigy.net.mx.

Computers 101. Valerie Jennings offers help with computer glitches, hardware and software programming and viruses. Also designs Web sites, and replaces memory. Rancho Margarita #2. **130-3832.**

Shari Reynolds comes highly recommended as a designer of Web pages. shari@redindigo.com.

Araiz – Punto com repairs computers and printers. Ancha de San Antonio #119, on the right side, at Stirling Dickinson. **154-7217.**

Charles Miller is a computer consultant who has a useful weekly column in *Atencion*. faq@smaguru.com.

CyberMacs, in Queretaro, is authorized to do warranty repairs and has supplies and equipment. The owner is Pedro Suarez. Avenida de Olmo #25, close to CostCo. Open 9:00 a.m.-2:00 p.m.; 4:00 p.m.-7:00 p.m. **01-442-212-3747.**

Instruction

Biblioteca's Computer Center. Ask at the front desk for a class schedule. The center is open weekdays, 10:00 a.m.-2:00 p.m.; 4:00 p.m.-7:00 p.m.; Saturday, 10:00 a.m.-2:00 p.m. Insurgentes #25.

Computers

Sarah Berges teaches the basics of Internet communications including the downloading of images, at the Computer Center. The cost for a 2-day weekend program is $990 pesos, including materials. To register, contact Jo Brenzo. Mesones #57. **152-2816.**

Internet Cafes

Internet cafes are all over town, in every neighborhood. Two of the most popular are Café etc. and Punto G.

Café etc. is a wonderful spot to hang out. In the small outdoor garden you'll usually find friendly people to chat with. The Internet room has 6 computers. The café has lots of great jazz and an inventory of 4,000 CDs that sell for as little as $35 pesos. They serve marvelous coffee from Chiapas and luncheon treats. Coffee sold by the pound is the best coffee bargain in San Miguel. Relox #37, below Insurgentes.
154-8636.

Punto G is an eccentric Internet entertainment center. The area in front of the high-speed work stations (1024 kbps) features tall glass Egyptian water pipes on round aluminum tables. Games, such as dominoes and backgammon are encouraged. Long distance telephone service is available. Coffee, espresso, cappuccino and juices are served, along with light snacks. At the entrance is an outlet for San Miguel sandals. Hidalgo #23. **152-1619.**

Living in San Miguel

EMERGENCY NUMBERS

Hospital Civil is the hospital of choice for many residents in an emergency. They say the emergency room is professionally staffed 24 hours a day. Relox #56. **152-0045** and **152-6015**.

Medical Emergencies: **152-0911**.

Red Cross Ambulance (24-hour service): **152-1616**, **152-4225**, **152-4121**.

Hospital de la Fe (24-hours, medical emergencies): **152-2545**.

Fire Department: **152-2888**.

Town Police: **152-0022**.

Automobile Emergencies:
Green Angel. 8:00 a.m.-8:00 p.m. **01 (800) 903-9200**.
Towing Service: **152-0660**.

Electrical Emergencies 152-7393
Gas Emergencies 152-0228
Water 152-4429
Cable TV 152-1942, 152-3442, 152-1145.

American Consulate Emergency Number 152-0068.

Reporting Lost or Stolen Credit Cards

American Express   01-800-504-0400
Master Card   01-800-307-7309
Visa   01-800-847-2911

FOOD AND WATER

Bakeries
The sensuous aroma of freshly-baked bread will propel you into one of the many bakeries that are in every neighborhood. A loaf of bread, a few rolls, cookies and pastry, will come to around $30 pesos. The treat of picking up the tongs and putting selections on the round aluminum tray.

Panderia El Maple is called the Canadian bakery in honor of the maple leaf sign at the entrance. Superb flour-dusted rolls and delicious sweet goods. Many residents rate it the town's best bakery in town. Open at 10:00 a.m. Salida de Ceyala, across from TELMEX.

La Colmena, also called the "blue doors," is a popular bakery. In addition to traditional bakery items, they sell empanadas, tasty appetizers of flaky half-oval crusts filled with tuna or cheese. They can be frozen. Open Monday, 8:30 a.m.-2:00 p.m. and 5:00 p.m-9:00 p.m.; Tuesday through Saturday, 6:00 a.m.-2:00 p.m.; Sunday, 6:00 a.m.-9:00 a.m. Reloj #21. **152-1422.**

La Buena Vida sells breads, muffins, rolls and cookies and excellent French bread. It's also a friendly spot to have snacks in the courtyard. Open Monday through Saturday, 8:00 a.m.-5:00 p.m. H. Macias #72, across the street from the Bellas Artes. **152-2211.**

Groceries
Gigante, the *supermercado* up the hill from town on the road to Queretaro is where almost everyone shops.

Living in San Miguel

The streets are best traversed by buses ($4 pesos) that make frequent trips, starting from the eastside of the Civic Plaza. Coming home with a load of groceries is a breeze. Cabs wait outside Gigante to take you to your door for $20 pesos. Gigante accepts credit cards.

Four stores in town are stocked with U.S. brands. They will have what you need.

Espino's has the style of a supermarket, and a good selection of wine and liquor. Open daily 8:30 a.m.-8:00 p.m.; Sunday, 8:00 a.m.-5:00 p.m. Codo #36, at the intersection of Zacateros.

Bonanza is centrally located, just below the Civic Plaza. Open daily 8:00 a.m.-8:00 p.m.; Sunday, 8:00 a.m.-5:00 p.m. Mesones #43.

Carey's is considered a bit expensive. It stocks hard-to-find brands, such as Minute Maid juice, Betty Crocker potatoes, Land O' Lake butter, Toll House chocolate chips and Tilamook cheese. Ancha de San Antonio #75, across from Hotel Aristos. **152-2038.**

El Tomate, next door to Espino's, has a wonderful assortment of fresh fruit, vegetables, fresh herbs and breads. Codo #36-B.

Washing Fruits and Vegetables

Most foreigners stay on the safe side and wash fruits and vegetables in *microbicida*, iodine drops available in most groceries. A common brand is Microdyn. Tomatoes, vegetables, and particularly lettuce, are soaked for 15 minutes in a large bowl of water with a few drops of Microdyn to vanish all traces of germs or insecticides. Purists suggest that even melons and avocados should be soaked because the knife, inserted into the skin, can "infect" the fruit. Leave time for items to drip dry.

Food and Water

Alternatives to iodine drops are white vinegar or laundry bleach, such as Clorox. White vinegar was recommended as a disinfectant by infectious disease specialist. Recommended are a few tablespoons of vinegar for each liter of water. For Clorox, a tablespoon should be added to a sink full of water. Suggested soaking time is 20 minutes.

Water, Bottled

Some residents use water straight from the tap; most are more protective. Some say the water's okay, but it's loaded with chlorine, which tastes terrible. Others say the water's okay but the gunk sticking to the ancient, corroded pipes makes it undrinkable.

Town water comes from 14 city wells, all of which are tested for purity on a regular basis. The problem is the underground distribution system that passes close-by ancient sewer lines.

Most *Norte Americanos* opt for bottled water to be on the safe side. Or, as is the case in many homes, hotels and bed and breakfasts, a water purification system covers the premises.

Bottled water can be scheduled for delivery. The 2.5 liter plastic bottles are a heavy lift for most women. Bottled water is available in most of the *bodegas*; return an empty bottle when you buy a full one. For convenience in pouring you should have a pump; they are available in most markets and grocery stores.

Water Purification

Water purification systems cover all household water, thus avoiding the need for the big bottles of clean water. Purification systems use 4-way carbon filters and ultraviolet beams to treat germs, bacteria and other impurities.

Many residents put a cup of Cloro in the water tank every so often to keep the pipes clean. Another approach for cleaning pipes is to install a filter on the water tanks (US$50 at Home Depot.)

Ivan Schuster is recommended for installing water purification systems. The cost is around US$500, plus US$500 for a pump. **154-8970** or, **044-415-149-3021.**

Monarca is a water purification system that uses a tube of colloidal silver pellets in the water tank or cistern to kill bacteria and parasites. The water purifier is guaranteed to last for 2 years. For installation call **152-3991.** The system is also available at **Don Pedro**, Ancha de San Antonio #123, at Guadiana. **152-1714.**

Water Testing
Hospital de la Fe sends water samples out for testing. The sample is placed in a paper cup provided by the hospital. Submitting the sample get an estimate of how long it takes to get the results. The hospital gives you a letter describing water quality. Libramiento #43. **152-2233, 152-2320** or **152-2329.**

Water Conservation
Water is a precious commodity in San Miguel and many residents are concerned that the town's rapid growth will outstrip its water supply. The key to insuring that water will be available is *conservation*. We all must be careful in our use of water. Don't keep water taps running and don't over-water your garden.

GARDENING AND GARDEN DESIGN

Soil is sold around town in bags that drape off donkeys' backs. Residents say it's unwise to buy from the street vendors because the soil is poor quality and it can be filled with insects. Better quality soil can be purchased at nurseries, such as those on Ancha de San Antonio, and on the road to the bus station.

Candelaria, which is held the first week in February in Benito Juarez Park, is the best place to furnish your patio or rooftop. Plant sellers from all over Mexico come to the park. Acres of flowers and trees provide a riot of color. Wheelbarrows and truckers are readily available to trek your purchases to your home. Otherwise, rely on several well-regarded nurseries

Nurseries
Vivero Primavera is in a small outdoor area at Salida a Celaya #32. They are well stocked with healthy, colorful plants and trees. Soil is also available.

Floriade is a large nursery near Hospital de la Fe, on Libramiento. The nursery can be seen from the road. In addition to potting soil they also stock commercial fertilizer, plant food, and peat moss.

Two large nurseries are on Salida de Celaya. One is on the right side as you leave town, in back of Diseno Antiguo. Further down Salida de Celaya on the left is a larger nursery. It's just before the Pemex station at the Glorieta.

Ceramic Pots

In purchasing unadorned pots, stay away from the yellow colored pots because they are fragile. The darker red pots have been fired longer and are stronger.

If you need a lot of ceramic pots, it's worth a trip to Dolores Hidalgo (Rte. 51), about 40 minutes from town on an excellent road. Medium sized ceramic pots cost about US$16. They are sold in many locations on both sides of the road as you approach the town.

Garden Design

Anado McLaughlin has created many beautiful gardens in San Miguel. He's from San Francisco and has a great eye for detail. His talented work crew is from La Cieneguita. bearbeing@unisono.net.mx. **155-8055.**

Carlos Ramirez Galvan is a master craftsman and artist who designs spectacular mosaic fountains, distinctive brick walls and patios and decorative outdoor metalwork. His sculpture, made from found objects, is both amusing and finely crafted. He can be contacted through Anado McLauchlin. **155-8055.**

Alfonso Alarcon is reported to be highly professional. He's designed gardens for some of the "best" houses here and he is considered to be a joy to work with. Cuadrante #6. **152-7754.**

ManRey Silva is also highly recommended. He lives in Pozos but works in San Miguel. **442-205-0811.**

Tim Wacher is considered to be responsible, careful and reasonable in pricing, but he has strong opinions. Perhaps that's a plus. **154-4746.**

GAY LIFE IN SAN MIGUEL

San Miguel's cultural, entertainment and real estate scenes are enlivened by the significant numbers of gays in town. Yet venues specifically patronized by gays don't seem to exist.

Most of the entertainment for the older crowd is provided in their homes, reflecting the elegant, private social life of gays in the 1940s.

Many unattached gays say they feel comfortable in the cantinas, the watering holes for local Mexican men. The cantinas can get pretty raucous and drunken, so they should be selected carefully. The cantina at the corner of Insurgentes and Hildago is reported to be particularly friendly and has a hospitable bartender during the day. The night crowd is a little too rough.

Club 27 welcomes gays on the third Wednesday of the month. To participate in the good times you must arrive fairly late; the revelry doesn't get started much before midnight. Hildago #27.

Younger gays patronize the popular bars and jazz joints. **Pancho and Lefty's** "La Lounge," upstairs in the late evening hours. Mesones #99.

Limerick Pub is a crowded, noisy and friendly bar with appropriate Irish décor. Umaran #24.

La Cucaracha is raucous well into the early morning hours. Zacateros #22.

Living in San Miguel

Le Petit Bar has an international clientele and is popular with the young as well as the more mature. Hernandez Macias #95.

En Agua is last on the list because it is often the final stop in a night of revelry. Jesus #19.

GOVERNMENT SERVICES and POLICE

San Miguel's 29-year-old mayor, Luis Alberto Villareal, is widely admired for putting civic funds to work to beautify the town and upgrade streets, sewers and water pipes. He has been successful in attracting funds from Mexico City for his public works projects.

The town budget is U.S. $21 million; 85% comes from state and federal allocations. The federal government imposes a hidden 15% value-added sales tax.

The mayor was elected in October, 2003 for a 3-year limited term. Some say he is being groomed to run for governor of Guanajuanto and then the Presidency.

The new County Institute of Information Access provides information on civic projects on its Web site at www.sanmiguelallende.gob.mx/transparencia.

City Hall, on the north side of the Jardin in Centro, is expected to move all of its 500 employees to a nearly-completed government complex on the road to Querétaro, in early 2005. The old city hall building will become a museum.

The mayor's director of foreign affairs, Christopher Finkelstein, is the go-to official for problems. He is considered to be available and responsive. His office is in City Hall, first floor on the left. E-mail: foreign_affairs_sma@yahoo.com.mx. **Tel. 152-0001,** extension **123.**

Living in San Miguel

Identification Cards

Starting early in 2005, the town will be providing on a voluntary basis photo ID cards for residents for a cost of $450 pesos. Imbedded computer chips can contain the name of your doctor, attorney and emergency numbers in case of an accident. The card can also show any allergies and your blood type.

Police and Security

San Miguel is considered to be a safe place to live. But it's comforting to know who to call on the off chance that you become a crime victim. The local police are not responsible for investigating criminal behavior; they are "preventive" officers.

In crime situations the appropriate contact is the *Ministerio Publico*, equivalent to the District Attorney's Office in the U.S. This is a special police force that investigates crimes. The Ministerio is on Calle Esparza, Oteo #17. **154-9451** and **154-9452**.

English-speaking Police Officer

If you need to call the police to report a robbery, noise complaint or other disturbance you may want to speak with an English-speaking officer. **Jose Francisco Mora Hernandez. 152-0022.**

Domestic Violence

CENAVI (Center of Attention for Domestic Violence) is a part of the government family ministry (DIF) and handles domestic violence cases. **152-3380.**

CASA (Center for the Adolescents) works with teenagers and women who have been abused. **154-6060.**

Municipal Institute of Women also offers support. **152-0001 ext. 141.**

GUESTS Ð WHERE TO STAY

When friends are planning to visit, they may ask for recommendations on where to stay. With the dozens of choices, all dutifully listed in other guides, this abbreviated list suggests several that are particularly friendly and exude the atmosphere and charm of San Miguel. Your choice will probably be determined in part by proximity to your home.

Casa de Liza is for guests who want sybaritic luxury. This is probably the most sumptuous inn in San Miguel. The meticulously restored colonial estate has exquisite grounds. Each casita or suite is distinctive and furnished with antiques. www.casaliza.com Bajada del Chorro #7. E-mail casaliza@prodigy.net.mx. **152-0352.**

Casa Luna Bed & Breakfast is in the moderate range (US$150 a night.) Lush landscaping and terraces for cocktails, in a restored 18th century villa. No two rooms are alike. Pila Seca #11. Internet reservations at www.casaluna.com. **152-1117.**

La Mansion del Bosque is a reasonably priced, delightfully eccentric inn where long-time proprietor Ruth Hyba is the gracious and accommodating host. The courtyard is festooned with flowers. Many rooms have private terraces. No two rooms are alike. Double rooms, with two meals, cost around US$90. Aldama #65. Reserve by e-mail at manruth@unisono.net.mx. **152-0277.**

Living in San Miguel

Villa Scorpio has a gorgeous rooftop with fabulous views and a hot tub. The rooms, all distinctly different, have traditional Mexican décor. Double rooms start at US$100. Quebrada #93. **152-7575.**

Las Terrazas San Miguel is a superbly managed Inn. Suites feature private patios with fountains. Murray Freidman and Greg Johnson are the congenial hosts. Santo Domingo #3, www.terrazassanmiguel.com **152-5028.**

HEATING AND FIREWOOD

Heating

Yes, it gets cold in San Miguel and when the season starts in November there's lots of chatter about how to stay warm.

Many residents like lava rock fire places. These are rocks or cement that have been burned to resemble logs. Lighted by a gas jet in a fireplace, they throw off lots of heat and give an attractive glow.

Alternatives are portable oil-filled or gas heaters. Ideally gas heaters should be put in the fireplace so that fumes go up the chimney. A small tank of gas costs $70 pesos and normally lasts about 3 months.

Be extremely careful in using un-vented gas heaters. They should only be used in well-ventilated rooms and not be left on all night. Last season two young girls died from lack of oxygen when they left the heater on all night.

Ferreteria Don Pedro has many styles of gas heaters that turn off automatically if the room lacks oxygen. The mid-range price is about $1,200 pesos.

Don Pedro is also universally recommended for its full line of hardware and fixtures, including lighting, wrenches and pipes. His tile and plumbing business next door sells Koehler products. Don Pedro's winning smile and gracious personality make him a favorite.

Living in San Miguel

Open weekdays, 8:00 a.m.-5:00 p.m.; Saturday, 8:00 a.m.-2:00 p.m. The store is near OXXO, in a pinkish building beyond the Instituto, just before SPASMA. Ancha de San Antonio #123. **152-2742** and **152-1714.**

Firewood

It's difficult to find firewood in San Miguel. Many eco-sensitive residents have converted their fireplaces to gas to protect what's left of the much deforested countryside. In winter, picturesque donkeys come to town with firewood draped on their skinny torsos.

Some carpinters sell leftover wood, but you'll need to go and get it.

Alexa Fullerton has firewood for sale. She also boards horses and gives riding lessons.
152-2760.

Nathan is said to be a provider. **152-0419.**

HIRING HOUSEHOLD HELP

On the books, all labor is full-time, a 44-hour week. The minimum wage is $300 pesos a week, which is far from a living wage. The employer is obligated to pay 35% of an employee's wages for social security.

Firing an employee is difficult. It's called "liquidation." After a 3-month trial period, an employee is considered to be permanent. To "liquidate" an employee generally requires payment of 3-months' wages plus 20 days' pay for each year of service. In employment disputes the laws generally favor the employee.

Maids
Ideally, you'll be able to employ an experienced maid who's been with the landlord or former owner for years. If not, rely on friends and neighbors to recommend a suitable person. Maids are not considered a luxury; vacuum cleaners are rare and house cleaning is still done the old fashioned way, with mops, rags and brooms. Even if a vacuum is provided maids are often reluctant to use them.

Pay scales vary, but expect to pay about $100 pesos a day, which means about three to four hours. Full-time maids work 6 days a week for a salary of around $500 pesos. By tradition and law, household help receives a bonus in early December of two weeks wages.

Actually, employment of a maid is more complicated than you might imagine, if the legalities are followed. Maids are supposed to have contracts, written in

Living in San Miguel

Spanish. When you hire a full-time maid you should pay US$600 a year up front for social security; part-time service is pro rated. Generally the principal employee makes the payment. It's a good idea to comply with the requirements because if a maid becomes dissatisfied, government officials may become involved and you could be liable for a sizable severance package, plus penalties for noncompliance.

Electricians, Plumbers and Handymen

Abraham Campos Ortega an electrician and superb all around handyman. Repairs phones, hangs chandeliers, caulks windows, and fix fountains. He arrives on time with all the tools needed for any job. He speaks English. His fee of $350 pesos for 2 hours sounds expensive, but considering his competence and versatility he's worth it. **044-415-100-7718.**

Lalo is the plumber recommended by Casa Roberto. He's polite and reasonably priced. He needs several days' notice. **044-415-103-1568.**

Roberto doesn't speak English but he understands plumbing problems. He's honest and reliable; prefers to fix rather than replace. **152-4393.**

Jaciento handles both plumbing and electrical problems. He understands English but doesn't speak it. **044-415-153-6642.**

Ebodio Ruiz Masonry and house painting, Juan Umaran #4, **152-7848.**

HOME FURNISHINGS

Home furnishings are probably the biggest "industry" in San Miguel. Everything from napkin rings to washing machines are in high demand. This section only scratches the surface. Described here are a few of the places that locals have recommended when they decorate their homes.

Appliances

Mosqueta has a full line of appliances, large and small. They may be priced slightly higher than in the big stores in Queretaro but you'll have the advantage of local service when needed. The store is considered highly reliable on the service front. Correo #34.and **152-0053.**

Appliance Repairs
Margarito Galvan is recommended for repairing appliances. **044-415-151-0468** or **120-8127.**

Ceramic Tile

Extraordinary bargains are available in Dolores Hidalgo. On the road leading into town on the right are several large tile centers.

Azulejos Talavera Cortes in downtown Dolores Hidalgo is the most frequently recommended factory. They feature superb quality, hand-pressed tiles in a wide range of colors and patterns. Tiles can be shipped to

Living in San Miguel

San Miguel at very reasonable prices. The store is on Calle Tabasco. www.talaveracortes.com.mx.
(418) 182-0900.

Fabrics

Elizabeth Noel has a fabulous collection of antique fabrics and collectible jewelry amassed from her many visits to remote villages in Guatemala. She also carries wall hangings, pillows, and table runners. San Rafael #4A, near San Juan de Dios Church. By appointment. **044-415-103-8856.**

Casas Colonials carries beautiful fabrics for upholstery and drapes, pillows and other decorative items. Canal #36. **152-0286** and **154-5731.**

Magnolia has a wide selection of colorful Mexican cotton fabrics for seat cushions and pillows for the modest price of $80 pesos a meter (39") and 91" wide. Recreo #2. **154-5705.**

El Nuevo Mundo specializes in Guatemalan products. Bedspreads can be used for pillow fabric. Prices are higher than at Magnolia but the material seems more substantial. The store is across from El Pegaso at San Francisco #17. **152-6180.**

Furniture

Grace's Sofas sells good looking, affordable sofas and loveseats handcrafted in San Miguel. Aldama #17.
153-2509.

Casa Diana in the village of Comonfort on the way to Celaya has a big selection of furniture housed in a yellow, one-story warehouse building. Be sure to also look in the large basement. The store makes high-quality furniture very quickly. They deliver orders over $2,000 pesos.

Home Furnishings

Bazar Romero & Flores is a huge, barn-like structure that carries an assortment of furniture and decorative items. Particularly notable are dozens of styles of chairs. Salida a Celaya #24. **152-2224.**

Casa Canal will make excellent quality furniture to your design. Pieces are considered fairly priced. Canal #3. **152-0479.**

C. Dewayne Youts has an extensive collection of stylish furniture and custom-made pieces in his enormous showroom. The excellent quality is matched with comparable prices. Calzada de la Aurora, just over the bridge. Open weekdays, 9:00 a.m.-6:00 p.m.; Saturday, 10:00 a.m.-4:00 p.m. **152-5481.**

Ferre, Art specializes in wrought iron (*hierro forjado*) furniture including lamps, tables, chairs, bedboards and chandeliers. The store will fabricate to your dimensions and design. They have a catalog of pieces. Reloj #81. **154-4905.**

Don Sholl for many years crafted high-level custom designed furniture for corporate clients on the Pacific Coast. His woodworking business is now in Guanajuato where he will build to your specifications. He also does wiring and plumbing to U.S. code standards. **01-473-101-5761** and **01-473-101-9252.**

Ramon Gonzalez will build custom-designed, inexpensive furniture. His shop is on the road to Dolores Hidalgo (Route 51.) Look for a furniture maker on the left, right at the big green overhead sign, before Dolores Hidalgo. Be sure to bring a sketch of what you want, with complete measurements. The work takes about 2 weeks. **01-418-183-2955.**

Outdoor Furniture

Patio sets and wrought iron furniture are on display in a large courtyard just beyond the Instituto de Allende.

Living in San Miguel

The prices seem a bit steep.

Casa Cohen has a good selection of wrought iron patio pieces. Mr. Cohen, the proprietor, is helpful and will refinish wrought iron tables at no extra cost. The store also carries bath and kitchen fixtures and handsome metal trays and serving utensils. Relox #12. **152-1434**.

Evo's has top quality, stylish patio furniture, with prices to match. Open Tuesday through Saturday, 10:00 a.m.-5:30 p.m. H. Macias #55, just beyond the Hotel Sautto. **152-081** and **152-8097**.

Glass Table Tops

Vidiios y Cristales de San Miguel, Ancha de San Antonio #117. **152-0359**.

La Muneca, Insurgentes #59. **154-4990**.

Housewares and Decorative Items

Sazon offers beautifully-designed dishes and linens. It's a real treat to visit this well-appointed store. Open Monday through Saturday, 10:00 a.m.-6:00 p.m.; Sunday, 11:00 a.m.-3:00 p.m. Correo #22. **154-7671**.

MITU is a boutique that carries exquisite accessories and antiques. Partners Anne-Marie Midy and Leslie Tung put together collections based on historic themes. Goods in the store change frequently. Open Tuesday through Friday, noon – 6:00 p.m.; Saturday, noon – 5:00 p.m. Sollano #32. **044-415-117-9431**.

Casa & Campo is a high-end, vaguely Victorian shop that sells furniture, fabrics, antiques and decorative objects. Recrero #98. **153-3298**.

Antigua Case Canela sells placemats, ceramics and decorative items. Umaran #20. **152-1880**.

Home Furnishings

Interior Design

Anne-Marie Midy has an international reputation in the design field. *House & Garden* magazine named her one of the 50 "New Tastemakers" in their January, 2005 issue for a home she designed in San Miguel. She has lived here for more than 5 years. **044-415-117-9431.**

Luba stages homes for successful resale, or just for a fresh new look that will transform your space. She is a former Santa Fe realtor and color consultant who will help present your home to its best advantage. Without new purchases, she creates furniture arrangements, color combinations and novel configurations of decorative objects. lluba@cybermatsa.com.mx. **154-9885.**

Tee Seals has helped many San Miguel residents design the interiors of their homes. She is available for consultations; her fee is based on orders placed. **152-4031.**

Jim Bolen is an interior designer from San Francisco who is establishing a practice here. **415-154-8026.**

Lighting Fixtures and Ceiling Fans

Casa Roberto is recommended for fixtures and fans and for fireplace jets for ceramic logs. Libramiento de Queretaro #35. **152-8620.**

Seamstress

Dolores Hernandez does sewing repairs on her industrial sewing machine. One of her 5 daughters speaks English. Colonia Guadalupe, Cri-Cri #20C. **154-4309.**

Living in San Miguel

Upholstery and Slip Covers

Sra. Gabriela Nieto has a thriving upholstery business. Her work is highly professional and service is fast. If you provide the fabric, 3 generously-sized floor pillows with zipper covers will cost about $190 pesos. Terraplen #25. **154-4121.**

Tapi Centro is well known for quality workmanship. Prog. Pila Seca #23. **91-415-253-24.**

Immigration

IMMIGRATION

The FM-T (Forma Migratoria para Turista)

Most of us start out in San Miguel as tourists. We pay little attention to the immigration form we filled out called an FM-T. Typically, the document permits a stay of 30 days. But for new residents who are spending more and more time in Mexico, the FM-T takes on greater importance. We have homes or leases on apartments and don't expect to return to the States or Canada within the specified time limits. Tourist visas can be extended at the immigration office.

Many residents have lived here for years without applying for Mexican residency. They routinely get visas that allow them to stay for 180 days. Every 6 months they return to the States and get their visas updated at the airport upon their return. For some the advantage is that they stay below the radar screen in terms of taxes on earnings generated here in Mexico. The only catch is that many Mexican immigration officers don't stamp the visa with the full 180 days. Then too, there's been talk that visa procedures may be revised to limit to 6 months a year the amount of time that holders of tourist visas can stay in the country.

Visa Extensions

For visa extensions go to the immigration office (*Delegacion Regional de Servicios Migratorios.*) It's a short distance beyond the traffic light at the Libramiento, beyond the bus station (Calzada de la Estacion.) In the

Living in San Miguel

office downstairs you'll be given the appropriate application form. Fill out the form and take it and your passport next door to have copies made of the form and each page of your passport. The cost for the visa extension is $210 pesos which must be paid at the Banorte or Banamax bank in El Centro. Then a trip back to immigration to get the official extension. The process usually takes the better part of a morning. The office is open from 9:00 a.m.-1:00 p.m.

The FM-3

Most new residents who plan to stay in Mexico for an extended period file for FM-3 residency status from the Mexican Government. With an FM-3 they can stay in Mexico for a year (it is renewable annually) and travel in and out of the country as many times as they choose. Also, the FM-3 allows new residents, for a 6-month period from the date of issuance, to bring their household goods into the country on a one-time basis, duty free. Getting the FM-3 is relatively easy. If you are shipping goods here it's best to wait until you know when you want to ship before applying.

The FM-3 can be obtained in the U.S. at Mexican consulates. The cost is about US$200 and takes about three days. In Mexico it takes two or three weeks. In either locale you will be asked to submit your passport and copies of every page of the passport, pictures, and copies of the latest 3 months of bank statements and brokerage accounts. Requirements frequently change, but some recent applicants applying in the United States have also been asked for statements from the local police indicating they have no criminal record.

In San Miguel, the bureaucratic paperwork is relatively painless. Many FM-3 applicants can do the paperwork themselves. They estimate the cost at about US$200. The necessary forms can be picked up at the Immigration Office at Calzada de la Estacion, beyond

Immigration

the bus station, straight ahead and shortly after the traffic light, on the left. After checking in at the Immigration Office and receiving the appropriate forms, the documents are taken to an office just beside Immigration. Clerks there will make the required copies of your passport, and fill in the forms for a fee of under US$10. Then a trek to a bank to pay the fee and back to Immigration. **152-2542.**

For the annual renewal of the FM-3, Immigration officials will want to see the title to your property here; or if you rent, a letter from your landlord stating that you have paid the rent and utilities.

To get an FM-3 in Mexico you may want to contact a Mexican specialist to help you through the process. **Patti Garcia** is an immigration expert who is universally recommended. For a modest fee she will file all the paperwork. Sollano #12. patgar5@yahoo.com. **152-0049**.

The FM-2

The other form of Mexican residency is the FM-2, which requires, in most cases, that you've held FM-3 status for 5 years. With an FM-2 you will avoid paying capital gains taxes on the appreciation of your residence.

Can I Earn Money?

The general answer is NO. If you come to Mexico on a visa you are not allowed to work; even the regular FM-3 residency permit precludes work. If you plan to work legally in San Miguel, your FM-3 form will need an authorization that is called an "expansion." Expansions are usually given for work with computers and English language instruction, and other specialties that are in short supply in Mexico.

Many Yankees skirt the system, but then it takes ingenuity to find customers or clients. A therapist in Boston will need to build a network of clients. Her

Living in San Miguel

sterling reputation in Boston will have no "legs" here. Perhaps through volunteer assignments and *pro bono* work the word will get around. But it would be rash to expect to use local earnings to pay the rent any time soon. There's also the risk that if the government determines you have been working illegally you can be subject to deportation.

While employment in the formal sector is risky and probably an unrealistic expectation, creating a business in San Miguel that employs local Mexicans is generally an easier matter. The FM-3 residency permit will need an "extension" that allows you to have a business. The business application must be approved. Tax forms must be completed and submitted every 2 months, or quarterly, depending on the situation. Tax on income earned in Mexico is a flat 15%.

In establishing a business, Immigration wants to be sure you're not taking jobs from Mexicans. A computer technician filed for a business permit and was turned down because there are computer experts here whose jobs could be in jeopardy. He then changed his job title to "office systems integration specialist" and was turned down again on the basis that now he would be taking the jobs of 4 Mexicans. Finally, using the title of "computer consultant", he convinced Immigration that his 30 years of computer experience would be engaged to help computer professionals in Mexico. And indeed over the years he's helped many Mexican computer technicians, using his network engineering experience on their behalf. He convinced the government that there's plenty of business for everyone and that he can help his Mexican colleagues stay up-to-date with modern technology.

KIDS' WORLD

Schools, Public and Private

Schooling is mandatory through the 6th grade, although any casual look at the numbers of very small children hawking gum and begging in the *Jardin* makes one wonder about enforcement.

Public school starts early, at age 18 months with maternal care, and moves to pre-kindergarten, kindergarten, and pre-first grade.

Most *Norte Americanos* avoid the public schools. They are on split sessions and do not provide an atmosphere for learning. Teachers are over-burdened and discipline is lacking. Children from the States find it difficult to adapt and harassment is a problem. Adolescents have the most difficult time. A blonde American teenage girl will be a magnet for the Mexican boys and thus be resented and rejected by her female classmates.

Parents are expected to participate in school activities. If they don't the child becomes an outcast. If a parent is absent at a school event this will be noted by the other parents and the attitude of the parents will be reflected in their children's' behavior toward the student without a parent present.

Most parents choose private schools; the tuition is a fraction of that for private schools in the States. There is a wide variety of choice – from a casual approach to

Living in San Miguel

learning Spanish with emphasis on cultural tours, to rigorous academic programs.

The prospect of having a child fluent in Spanish brings many parents to Mexico for a term or two at the pre-high school level. The bicultural experience is a life-long gift parents can give their children.

Many parents send their children to schools outside of San Miguel after they receive their 6th grade certificate. Many go to schools in Queretaro, Leon or to boarding school.

After high school most parents send their kids to college in the United States or Canada. University training in Guanajuato and Mexico City is as rigorous as it is in most American colleges, but for U.S.- oriented students who expect to make their lives in the States, an American degree is generally considered preferable. An American child who has lived in Mexico and is fluent in Spanish may have a slight edge in the college entrance process because colleges seek diversity and special skills and talents.

Many private schools are Catholic. They charge about US$75 a month for a full 12 months, plus double payments in December and June. Summer vacation is 6 weeks. Grade levels are equivalent to those in the States.

Jose Vasconcelos is considered to be the most rigorous private school. It takes students through the 9th grade. It's completely bilingual, with 3 hours in English and 3 hours in Spanish each day. Less than 20 students in the class. The cost is around US$3,500 per year, plus uniforms. The school is considered "snobbish" and discipline is difficult because the student body reflects the San Miguel hierarchy. Barrio de Obraje, north of Cazada de la Luz. **152-1869.**

Kids

Victoria Robbins is particularly strong in math and history. The school is exceptionally casual and there are no uniforms. It specializes in students who are having academic difficulties and who can't fit into Mexican schools. Tutors provide one-on-one teaching, which goes from 7th the 10th grade. After 10th grade, Texas Tech provides correspondence courses that are given at the school. Tuition is around US$270 a month. Frederico Ledesma (Colonia Guadalupe.) **152-0287.**

Atabal is a bilingual school based on the Montessori method. Tuition is US$250 a month. It's a trek out to Los Frailes, but mothers arrange car pools. The school is adding grade levels and will eventually go through grade 6. **415-155-8248.**

Los Charcos Waldorf Kinder and Primary School. The school has a country campus, and emphasizes a holistic education. www.colegiowaldorf_sma.tripod.com. **154-7869.**

Two bilingual schools are considered to be excellent choices for students who are here temporarily. They are geared to the American system and accept students for as short a time as one month.

Centro Bilingual of San Miguel teaches in Spanish but is lenient with new students who have limited comprehension. The approach is to have 4 hours of Spanish and then students are taken on field trips. Math and science are not part of the curriculum. The school has a well-regarded summer camp and a Christmas Spanish day camp. Contact Sara Murillo. Correo #46. **152-5400.**

Centro Mexicano de Lengua y Cultura has a multi-cultural program for children ages 3 through 12. Morning classes from 9:00 a.m.-1:00 p.m. Program includes Spanish, arts and crafts, cooking, games and excursions. Contact Josefina Hernandez. **152-0763.**

Living in San Miguel

Schools That Teach in Spanish

Colegio Fray Pedro de Gante, off Calle de Aurora. In this K through 12 school, the teachers are Catholic madres. Tuition is US$120 a month, plus books and uniforms. One American parent said the school is more advanced in math than U.S. schools. Computer classes, physical education and team sports are held twice a week. It's in an outlying location; many mothers arrange with a taxi driver to pickup and deliver their children. Avenida Primero de Mayo #4. Col. Aurora. fpgante@prodigy.net.mx. **152-241.**

Instituto de Las Casas is a small, excellent school, pre-K through 12. Early grades meet in the morning; upper grades in the afternoon. Tuition is about $800 pesos a month, plus extras including 3 sets of uniforms. Santo Domingo #1. **152-1374**

KIDS' ACTIVITIES

Mothers with pre-teenagers and those a bit older, caution that it's important to have a structured after-school life for your kids. Just as in the States, children with time on their hands can get in trouble or travel in an undesirable crowd. There are probably as many educational and leisure time outlets for kids here as there are in the States. Children with artistic or sports interests have dozens of areas to explore. Art and music classes and sports, such as horseback riding, are considerably less expensive here. San Miguel offers the opportunity for your children to broaden their horizons by trying new sports and artistic endeavors.

SPORTS

Malanquin Country Club has a month-long summer camp, with sports, arts and field trips. www.malanquin.com **152-0516** and **154-8210.**

Kids

Baseball
Baseball for kids age 8 and above is played on Saturday morning at 10:00 a.m. on a lot behind Gigante.

Basketball
Benito Juarez Park has after school basketball. Just show up and pre-teens (generally ages 9 to 12) will be put on the team. Competition games are played on Sunday morning.

Computer Games
Dark Place is the name pre-teens and teenagers call this dimly-lighted hole in the wall that's a particular magnet for boys. The feature is X Boxes and related console video games such as Play Station II, Game Cube and other hot items. Parents find the place potentially threatening for their teenage boys, but the allure is such that their kids go there anyway. It's located near the end of Hildago, near Calzada de la Luz, on the left. It's formal name is Salon de Fiestas Rocio. Hildago #82.

Horseback Riding
Coyote Canyon Adventures conducts a summer riding program for kids. **154-4193**, or cell: **044-415-153-5005**.

Swimming
Santo Domingo Sports Club has a popular year-round afternoon swimming program. Classes for children ages 4 to 13, from 4:00 p.m.-6:00 p.m. Annual subscription US$200. $35 pesos per class. Santo Domingo #55. **154-7545**

Tennis
Hotel Posada de la Aldea has afternoon children's programs. The pro is Mauricio Chauvet. Ancha de San Antonio #15. **154-5179**.

Living in San Miguel

Water Slides

XOTE is a water wonderland for kids and a day outing that will delight the family. This well-run facility is on the road to Dolores Hidalgo, before the Escondido Spa and La Gruta hot springs. Five pools, each with carefully monitored slides, landscaped hills, lots of shade trees and lush grass. You can bring your own food and prepare it on their grills. Purchased food is reasonably priced. Turn left at the Taboada sign and go to the top of the hill.

Art and Music Classes

ABCD is a pre-school art program that's taught in English. Salida a Celaya #81. **152-4477.**

Biblioteca has free storytelling and classes for kids in origami and painting. Insurgentes #25. **152-0293.**

Casa de la Cultura teaches dance, guitar, piano, violin and painting to children generally ages 8 and up. Bajada del Chorro #4. **154-5670.**

Escuela de Arte Canek has classes for children in watercolor, drawing, crafts and piano. Calle San Martin #20, Col San Antonio. **152-4520.**

El Recreo offers classes for children age 6 though teenage. The schedule includes lessons in jazz dance, Mexican dances, classical ballet, karate, piano and violin, to name just a few. Also children's theater. Recreo #4.**152-0131.** For full schedule see recreosm@prodigy.net.mx.

Rebecca Peterson conducts bilingual art classes for kids. The monthly rate is $150 pesos for 1° hour class, including materials. Pre-registration required. Calle Arroyo del Atascadero #3A mexrebe@yahoo.com. **154-7010.**

Kids

Meynarda Morales has art classes for young children off a sun-filled courtyard at Hidalgo #78. Morning and afternoon sessions, year round, including ceramics and weaving. Classes are in Spanish. $46 pesos an hour. **152-5268.**

Ceramics
Joan Elena Goldberg teaches at **The Little Clay School**, San Antonio Abad #36. Pre-registration required. **152-844.**

Guitar
David Bar-Chai All levels and ages welcome. **154-9239.**

Papier Mache
Lisa Simms conducts workshops where she teaches papier mache techniques. Kids create masks, puppets and sculpture. Tuesday and Thursday, 3:00 p.m.-4:45 p.m. **152-5152.**

Spanish
Centro Bilingual of San Miguel has an excellent Spanish summer day camp for kids. www.geocities.com/centrobilingue. To register contact Sara Murillo. Correo #46. **152-5400.**

Living in San Miguel

LAUNDRIES AND DRY CLEANERS

Laundries are available in all neighborhoods. Bring your laundry bag in the morning for afternoon pickup. Aside from having to schlep the bag (pick-up and delivery is available but you have to be home) the service is amazing. Your items will be neatly folded, and encased in clear plastic, with almost Origami perfection.

Whether it's the chlorine in the water, the bleaching additives used by the laundry or the temperature of the water, clothes sent to laundries here seem to disintegrate rapidly. Fragile lingerie should be washed at home. To cut down on wear and tear ask that no bleach (*cloro*) be used.

Tintoreria Franco Lavanderia is considered a top choice. They offer free pickup and delivery. They also clean rugs, draperies and curtains. On Ancha San Antonio, #15-A, at Zacateros. **152-4362 or 152-5377.**

La Pila, Also dry cleaning. Open weekdays 9:00 a.m.-7:00 p.m.; Saturdays 9:00 a.m.-2:00 p.m. Jesus #25. **152-5810**.

Express Laundry has same-day pickup and delivery. Carlos is dependable; he never loses items and they're exactly folded *perfecto*. Canal #127. **152-7086.**

Dry Cleaning

Paris is among the most recommended dry cleaners. They also do laundry and provide pickup and delivery service. Mesones #91. **152-0219** and **152-4113.**

Tintorerias del Bajio, S.A. de C.V. Pedro Nuñez de la Rioja #111, Celaya, Gto., **(461) 612-8876**. Free Pickup and Delivery.

MEASUREMENT CONVERSIONS

Miles and Kilometers:
One mile = 1.61 kilometers;
One kilometer = 0.62 miles.
Convert kilometers to miles, multiply by 0.6.

Yards/inches to Meters:
One yard = 0.91 meters;
One meter = 39.37 inches.

Pounds to Kilograms:
One pound = 0.37 kilograms;
One kilogram = 2.2 pounds.

Ounces to Grams, multiply by 28;
Grams to Ounces, multiply by 0.035.

Gallons to Liters:
One gallon = 3.785 liters;
10 liters = 2.46 gallons.

Hectacre = 2.47 acres

Oven Temperature Conversions
Temperature dials on Mexican ovens are expressed in Centigrade; from 100 degrees to 250 degrees. "Asar" means broiler. Centigrade to Fahrenheit conversions: 110C = 225F; 150C = 300F; 200C = 375F; 230C = 450F; 260C = 500F.

Living in San Miguel

You may have noticed that it takes longer to boil vegetables in San Miguel. That's because water boils at a lower temperature in high elevations. The boiling point of water at sea level is 212 degrees Farenheit or 100 degrees Celsius. At 5,000 feet it's 203 degrees Farenheit or 98 degrees Celsius, and at 7,500 feet it's 198 degrees Farenheit or 92 degrees Celsius. To compensate for high elevations (San Miguel is about 6,500 feet) add 15-20 degrees to the recipe's for oven temperature and a few minutes for food cooked on the burners.

Converting Fahrenheit to Celsius
Fahrenheit to Celsius: Subtract 32 from the Fahrenheit temperature, multiply by 5, divide by 9.

Celsius to Fahrenheit: Multiply the Celsius temperature by 9, divide by 5 and add 32.

Medical

THE MEDICAL SCENE

Many residents believe that health care in Mexico is comparable to that in the States. Doctors in Mexico City and Querétaro are thought to be on a par with their stateside counterparts and the cost of care is a fraction of that in the United States. Many of the doctors at Hospital de la Fe were trained at top U.S. hospitals and spent years in private practice in the States.

If you are concerned about a major health problem and would prefer to seek treatment in the United States you should consider enrolling in a Medivac program.

Medical Air Services Association (MASA) is a membership organization that provides air evacuation to a U.S treatment center and air service back to Mexico. The cost to join for a resident of Mexico is US$240 a year for one person; US$360 for a family. www.masamexico.com. **152-4444**.

Hospitals

Hospital de la Fe, the hospital used by most foreigners, is located at the traffic light on the road to Dolores Hidalgo. Libramiento #43. For non-emergencies and appointments, call **152-2233, 152-2320** or **152-2329**. Emergency number is **152-2545**.

Hospital Civil is recommended by many residents for emergency care. Its round-the-clock emergency room staff is considered the best in town. Reloj #56. **152-0045** or **152-6015**.

Living in San Miguel

Medical Doctors

Dr. Silvia Azcarate specializes in general medicine, nutrition and minor surgery. She is thorough and conservative in prescribing medication. She's the doctor of choice for many foreigners. Office hours on weekdays, 10:30 a.m.1:30 p.m.; 5:00 p.m.-7:00 p.m. She makes house calls. Codo 9-A. **152-1944**.

Dr. Chris Ramaglia is highly recommended by the foreign community. His practice is general medicine. Pica Seca #53. **152-2111**.

Dr. Salvador Quiroz is a popular doctor with the expat community. He makes house calls. Hospital de la Fe. **152-2233**.

Dr. Arturo Barrera is considered to be a superb diagnostician. Some say his bedside manner is a bit rough. Hospital de la Fe. **152-2233**.

Dr. Jorge A Martiniez is also recommended by residents. He makes house calls. He can be reached on his cell: **044-415-153-8832**.

Dr. Jorge Alvarez is a cardiologist. He can be helpful in checking pacemakers. Hospital de la Fe, **152-2233**.

Ob-Gyn
Dr. Sandra Ramirez is well-regarded and the ob-gyn of choice for many expats. Call Hospital de la Fe at **152-2233**.

Dr. Hugo Rosas is considered to be kind, gentle and competent. Patients feel well taken care of. However, he doesn't speak English. Hospital de la Fe. For an appointment call **152-2233**.

Medical

Ear, Nose and Throat
Dr. Lilian Hernandez is highly recommended by patients with ENT problems. Hospital de la Fe. **152-2233.**

Dermatology
Dr. Blanca Farias. Umaran #20B, altos. **152-2321.**

Opthalmology
Drs. Francisco Velazquez and **Patricia Sobrevilla** treat cataracts, glaucoma and macular degeneration. Appointments through the Hospital de la Fe. **152-2233.**

Plastic Surgeons
Plastic surgery is a big business in San Miguel. Many stateside residents come down for the surgery since it is considerably less expensive here.

Dr. Carlos Berrera is a fully-certified plastic surgeon who practices in Celaya but comes to San Miguel several days a week. The all-inclusive US$4,000 price for a face lift includes consultation, medical tests, travel to and from Celaya, surgery, and 2 nights in the Celaya hospital. The doctor comes to San Miguel 10 days after surgery to remove the stitches. He does only one surgery a day, on Monday, Tuesday and Wednesday. **461-613-6439** and **461-113-1496.**

Dr. Jorge de la Fuente offers a full line of plastic surgery procedures, including face lifts, liposuction, Botox and peels. Refugio Sur #39, in Colonial San Antonio. **152-2249**.

Dr. Manuel Velazquez, **Clinica La Joya**. Board- certified surgeons do laser resurfacing, microdermabrasion, and Botox. Appointments on Wednesdays. **01-461-613-4210.** www.lajoyaclinica.com.

Dr. Juan Bosco Ruiz-Padilla, MD, is a Board- certified plastic and reconstructive surgeon that does face lifts, eyelids, breast augmentation and reduction, tummy tucks, liposuction, hand surgery, and treatments for skin cancer. boscosur@cybermatsa.com.mx Potranca #29, Guadiana. **152-2172.**

Dentists

Dr. Laura Elias Urdapileta, know as Doctor Laura, is the dentist of choice for many expats. Open weekdays, 9:00 a.m.-8:00 p.m. San Jorge #12. **152-4330.**

Dr. Guadalupe Tejada Gomez is a highly- recommended dental surgeon, particularly for patients who've had bad work done elsewhere. She does expert reconstructive work. Salida a Celaya #22. **152-2065** and **154-5152.**

Dr. Elvira Cecelia Berrospe specializes in dental surgery, including extractions. Bilingual. Discusses treatment thoroughly and calls the day after treatment to check on progress. She will also recommend a root canal specialist who comes to San Miguel from Queretaro. Hospital de la Fe. **152-2233** or **154-6474.**

Dr. Jesus Herrera, at the *Clinica Odontologica Especializada,* in Celaya, gets rave reviews. A professor of dentistry, many oldtimers go there "to avoid having work redone elsewhere." **461-612-1845**.

Dr. Alberto Salazar, DDS. Dental surgery, porcelain crowns, porcelain facing. Codo #9.
152-3608 or **152-2138.**

Drug Stores

Druggists in Mexico act as informal general medical practitioners. They diagnose common ailments, suggest remedies, write prescriptions and administer shots. A medical prescription is required for Valium and other "controlled substances." Most pharmacies are well-stocked with generic drugs but are sometimes short on brand name pharmaceuticals.

Medical

When receiving a prescription it's advisable to check the dosage and contents; sometimes drug stores fail to provide sufficient drugs for the recommended period of use.

Botica Agundis is the pharmacy of choice for many in the expat community. **Chelo**, the proprietor, is widely admired for her direct approach, astute diagnoses and effective remedies. Open every day, 10:30 a.m.-11:00 p.m. Canal #26, at the corner of H. Macias. **152-1198.**

Farmacia Guadalajara is part of a chain of hundreds of pharmacies in Mexico. It's well stocked and offers a 30% discount from listed drug prices. Open 24 hours and accepts credit cards. Ancha de San Antonio #13. **154-9047.**

Farmacia ISSEG is a small drugstore that is reputed to have the best prices on prescription drugs. On Mesones, next to Mesones #14.

Eyeglasses and Repairs

Optica San Miguel has certified optometrists who perform eye examinations. They carry a wide assortment of frames and they do eyeglass repairs. Juarez #7. **154-4546.**

Optica Allende provides efficient, friendly repair service. H. Macias #113.

Health Insurance

U.S. MediCare and supplemental policies such as AARP cannot be tapped in foreign countries. If you plan to return to the United States it's advisable to keep your Part B coverage intact.

Living in San Miguel

You might investigate private health insurers in the United States to see if they provide international coverage. Limited health insurance is available in Mexico but many residents go without insurance because the cost of medical care here is so much less than in the States.

Private health insurance generally does not cover drugs and medicine, unless you're in the hospital. When entering a hospital you will be asked to provide a credit card and the charges will be billed to you. It's your responsibility to go after reimbursements.

IMSS (*Instituto Mexicano del Seguro Social*) health insurance from the Mexican government is available to foreign residents who have FM-3 status. There are age restrictions and exclusions for previous medical conditions. Applicants must appear in person at the main office in Guanajuato. The cost is US$150-$250 a year depending on your age. For the first year there are a few exclusions, such as for asthma, allergies and arthritis.

Under the IMSS system you are assigned a local primary care doctor who will refer you to specialists as needed. Doctors will converse with you in Spanish, so if you're not fluent, bring a translator. Many residents use IMSS as a backup in case of emergencies.

Tilloglobe offers off-shore heath insurance with Lloyd's of London. The cost of coverage starts at about $50 per month. Options include medical emergencies and air ambulance.Contact information: www.tilloglobe.com or email Robert@tilloglobe.com.

Mexpro (Mexico Insurance Professionals) sells international health and air ambulance insurance through Global Medical Insurance. It has a $5 million cap. Price quotes for selected coverage can be obtained on the Internet at www.mexpro.com.

Medical

Hearing Aids/ Audiology

Guillermo Sanchez is a licensed audiologist who comes frequently to San Miguel from Mexico City to give hearing tests. Appointments can be scheduled through **Gordon Jett** at **152-2621**.

Homeopaths and Acupuncturists

Homeopaths and homeopathic remedies are popular in San Miguel. Many residents turn first to tincture of plants and other natural potions to cure common ailments. Mothers of small children find this is a particularly appealing approach.

Dr. Conchita Garcia Escobedo is a medical doctor who favors homeopathic remedies and she is highly regarded. She specializes in rehabilitation of facial paralysis and nerve problems. She uses electrode machines, hot packs and traction. Office hours are 8:00 a.m.-5:00 p.m. Mesones #62. **152-3793**.

Dr. Garcia Glez has a store chock full of intriguing vials of natural oils, potions and homeopathic remedies. Open Monday through Saturday, 10:00 a.m.-2:30 p.m.; 5:00 p.m.-8:15 p.m. Mesones #67. **152-0230**.

La Victoriana has a wide assortment of homeopathic remedies. The store offers a useful small booklet that describes dozens of items used to treat rashes, wounds, bruises and diarrhea, to name just a few. H. Macias #72, across from Bellas Artes. **152-6903**.

Dr. Cesar Gil Hoyos is a recommended acupuncturist and also a medical doctor. Potrero #8. **154-5111** or **044-415-149-7502**.

Lori Wilson is a U.S. licensed acupuncturist. She specializes in Japanese-style acupuncture and Chinese

Living in San Miguel

herbal medicine. She comes regularly to San Miguel from Guanajuato.
01-473-101-5761 and **01-473-101-9252.**

Reflexology
Linda Sorin is a New York trained reflexologist with 35 years experience in helathcare. Relexology uses acupressure on the feet to create deep relaxation, improve circulation and help the body's healing process. Patients report that it also eases pain from migraines and sciatica. Pipila #11, Colonia San Antonio. lindasorin@yahoo.com. **154-4069.**

MEDICAL SUPPORT SYSTEMS

San Miguel has several agencies that provide home care nurses, on a part-time or 24-hour basis, at a cost that is considerably lower than in the States. Much of the information here was gathered by the authors of *Our Caring Community*. This extremely valuable resource should be on every resident's bookshelf. It is widely available in bookstores.

Home Healthcare

Premium Home Health Care Providers has range of trained caregivers, from nurses and nursing aides, to companions for short- or long-term assistance. Qualified help is available for a handicapped child or impaired adult. Emergency care is also available. Salaries, depending on qualifications, range from US$120 to US$360 for a 40-hour week. The agency is managed by Robin Fell, a healthcare professional with many years experience in home healthcare.
www.premiumhomehealthcareproviders.com.mx.
E-mail robinfell@cybermatsa.com.mx. **152-5555.**

Twenty-Four Hour Care Services of Oscar de la Pena arranges nursing care, employing nurses associated with the Hospital de la Fe. The charge is $30 to $35 pesos an hour. E-mail emsm@unisono.net.mx.
154-6810.

Dr. Silvia Azcarate is a general practitioner who trains and supervises bilingual caregivers who are trained to give shots, check blood pressure and change surgical bandages; they are also available to run errands and chauffeur. Fees are $70 pesos per hour weekdays; $350 pesos for a 24-hour shift. Office open weekdays, 11:00 a.m.-1:30 p.m.; 5:00 p.m.-7:00 p.m. House calls every day. Codo 9, #A. **152-1944.**

Medical Equipment

St. Paul's Church provides in-home care products free of charge, including wheelchairs, crutches and canes. Open 10:00 a.m.-2:00 p.m. **152-0387** or, in emergencies, **152-4714.**

Ortopedia J. Ortiz has a wide variety of orthopedic equipment, including orthopedic shoes, crutches and corsets. Zacateros #41. **152-6004.**

Medical Alert System

Radio Shack sells a console and call pendant that will allow you to call, at the press of a button, up to four telephone numbers of friends or neighbors. The cost is between US$55 and US$65. Order a system, over the Internet at wwwradioshack.com. **152-2435.**

Making Final Arrangements

Twenty-Four Hour Association is a membership organization that handles the legal and funeral arrangements for their members. Members compile personal data concerning wills, executor and special instructions. The upfront fee covers the costs.

Cremation costs $6,300 pesos. Burials are $10,000 pesos. The group has been in existence since 1965. If you move or decide not to use the Association, the fee is refunded. Contact the Association's secretary, Bonnie Besnett. **152-3536,** or the treasurer, Melanie Nance. **152-6668** (evenings)

NIGHTLIFE AND ENTERTAINMENT

Tio Lucas. Live music every night. Excellent steaks and the ambiance is wonderful. Reservations needed, particularly on weekends. Mesones #103. **152-4998.**

Mama Mia's. Peruvian music, Wednesday and Saturday evenings. Umaran #8 **152-2063.**

Casa Payo. Argentine music on weekends. Zacateros #28. **152-7277.**

El Market Bistro. Live music, wonderful steaks, romantic outdoor patio. H. Macias #95. **152-3229**.

Finnegans Pub, Restaurant. Wide variety of musical offerings including traditional Irish music, guitars, gypsy soul and flamenco dance. Closed on Tuesday. Codo #7. **044-415-100-3525.**

Casa de Sierra Nevada. Sedate jazz and wine bar, Wednesday through Saturday, starting at 6:30 p.m. **152-7040, ext. 128-131.**

Limerick Pub is a noisy bar that's popular with the younger crowd. Umaran #24.

La Vida is a comfortable, down-home neighborhood hangout with a friendly bar and always someone to talk with. Large TV screen that features sports events. Host Anisetto has an infectious smile and always a warm welcome. Ancha de San Antonio #31, just up from the Instituto.

El Grito has a dance floor and a lively crowd of young people. It gets raucous on weekends.
Umaran #15. **152-0048.**

En Agua is for the super young hipsters in their early 20s. Late night scene. It's inconspicuous and easy to miss, with only a small sign. On Jesus, between #19 and #21, across the street from UMO.

La Cucaracha is another late night venue. The original bar was a hangout for Jack Kerouac and many of the other beatniks. Zacateros #22. **152-0196.**

La Carpa is an exciting new venue for nightlife. It's a community entertainment center in a bright red and lavender circus tent. Live performances include acrobats and Mexican vaudeville. It's a popular gathering spot that has verve and an energy field that's extraordinary. It is located on Calzada de la Aurora, the extension of Hidalgo, just across the bridge on the right.

Dancing

Mama Mia has free salsa classes on Wednesday evenings, from 7:00 p.m.-10:00 p.m. Umaran #8. **152-2063.**

Rincon Espanol presents Flamenco performances at shows on Saturday and Monday at 8:30 p.m., and on Sunday at 3:00 p.m. The restaurant's specialty is paella. Correo #29. **152-2984.**

El Ring is a lively venue for dancing on Thursday night. The strobe-lighted dance floor, black ceiling with gold light fixtures and huge seductive posters of famous dance scenes make it almost impossible not to take to the dance floor. Salsa classes on Thursday at 7:00 p.m.; after that, music from the 50s, 60s and 70s gives everyone a chance. Hidalgo #27.

Nightlife

Bovedas Bar has a dance floor. Free salsa classes on Friday, 6:00 p.m.-8:00 p.m. Open Thursday through Saturday, 6:00 p.m.-1:00 a.m. Sunday dancing from 5:00 p.m.-10:00 p.m. Tinajitas #24, Col. San Antonio, one street before Stirling Dickinson, at Refugio.

Movies

Villa Jacaranda presents classic American and international films. Weekly schedule is in *Atencion*. $60 pesos, includes a drink and popcorn. Usually presented at 7:30 p.m.; weekend matinees at 3:30 p.m. Aldama #53. **152-1015.**

Cinemateca at the Biblioteca's Santa Ana Theater presents a wide variety of movies of note. Weekly schedule in *Atencion*. Showings typically at 5:00 p.m. and 7:30 p.m. Insurgentes #25. **152-3094.**

Cinema Gemelos, behind the Gigante supermarket, shows both Mexican movies and U.S. films, generally of the "action" variety. Weekly attractions listed in *Atencion*. **152-6408.**

Movie Rentals

Block Busters, across from the Instituto, has a big selection of DVDs. They offer 3 films for 5 nights for $59 pesos. Ancha de San Antonio #7.

Netflix.com is a subscription service that sends DVDs three at a time, postage free. You create your own movie list from over 25,000 titles. No late fees and DVDs can be kept as long as you want. Subscription is US$18 a month. Check it out on the Internet at www.netflix.com.

Office Supplies

OFFICE SUPPLIES

San Miguel could really use a fully-stocked office supply store. Existing small stores lack inventory on such essentials as computer peripherals, paper and ink cartridges for copiers. If possible, stock up on your computer and paper needs at Office Max or Office Depot in Queretaro.

Bibiana Mora Orvananos is one of the better stocked stores. They will refill copy machine ink cartridges for about half the price ($120 pesos) of buying a new cartridge. Cartridges can be refilled 3 or 4 times. Open weekdays, 10:00 a.m.-8:00 p.m.; Saturday, 10:00 a.m.-2:00 p.m. Canal #59-A. **154-8003**.

MDT Computadoras, is around the corner from Bibiana (walking toward town.) They have the most complete inventory of ink cartridges. They also carry peripherals. Beneficencia #19. **152-5253**.

Papeleria Heros Insurgentes is a small store that's loaded with stationery, computer paper, ink cartridges and other office supplies. It's conveniently located at Juarez #25. **152-0138**.

Business Cards

Imprenta Martinez uses digital equipment. An English-speaking designer whizzes through the process, with you sitting beside him. He keeps going until you're satisfied. 100 cards, in color, cost $190 pesos; 200 cards

Living in San Miguel

are $280 pesos. Once the design is done you'll have the cards the next day. Nunez #18. **152-1361.**

PERSONAL CARE

SPAS, MASSAGE, HAIRSTYLING

One of the biggest "industries" in San Miguel is health and beauty. Every conceivable variety of treatment is available.

Spas

Patricia is recommended for her luxurious facial treatments and friendly presence. For pedicures, she tosses rose petals in the soaking water. Everyone involved is expert and congenial. Ladrillera #1, off Pila Seca. **154-8104.**

Casa de Sierra Nevada. Health and beauty center with massage, facial treatments, manicures and pedicures. By appointment only, Tuesday through Saturday, 9:30 a.m.-2:00 p.m.; 3:00 p.m.-6:30 p.m. Hospico #44. **152-7040** and **152-1895.**

Bambu Day Spa. Massage, body treatments, facials and a "Wellness for Life" clinic." Open weekdays, 9:00 a.m.-4:00 p.m.; Saturday, 10:00 a.m.-3:00 p.m. Ancha de San Antonia #15, Suite B, inside the Posada de la Aldea Hotel. **044-415-103-0240.**

El Quinto Sol dia Spa. Steam, sauna, detoxification. Specializes in hair treatments. Farolito #10, Col. Guadalupe. Call for an appointment. **152-1608.**

Living in San Miguel

Joyous Day Spa. Modern technology is used for microcurrent facials, microderm abrasion, and cellulite treatments. Also available are massages and clinical hypnotherapy. Joyous distributes Shaklee cosmetic products. Garita #16. Call for an appointment. **152-1213.**

The Reflex Center. Professional neuro-muscular and massage therapists. Also, hair styling, manicures, pedicures, and facials. Open every day. Sergio Ortega. Aparicio #48A. **154-6903.**

Massage

Ann Bowles is considered by many to be the best masseuse in town. She was on staff for many years at the Canyon Ranch spas. Her massages are extraordinary. **152-7861.**

Juana Ceballos Gonzalez. Reflexology, facial rejuvenation. Weekdays, 10:00 a.m.-5:00 p.m. **152-7761.**

Rhea's Massage. Flemish, Traeger, Shiatsu, Chi Nei Tsang, stone therapy. Canal #135A. Leave a message, 2:00 p.m.-4:30 p.m. at **152-8971.**

Energetic Balance through Reflexology. Certified practitioner **Martha Hernandez. 152-5578.**

Hair Styling

Salon and Spa de Robert is favored for hair styling and coloring. Facial and body treatments, manicures and pedicures are also available. Zacateros #83-A. **154-8188.**

Jose Marin is an expert hair stylist. His salon also does color, manicures and pedicures. Monday through

Personal Care

Saturday, 10:00 a.m.-2:00 p.m.; 4:00 p.m.-8:00 p.m. Nunez #14. **152-4771.**

Carmela is a popular spot for haircuts for men and women. Inside the courtyard at Canal #9. **152-1346.**

Bandala is another good place for haircuts for both men and women. This tiny shop is at H. Macias #62A, across from Hotel Sautto. No appointment needed.

Living in San Miguel

PETS IN SAN MIGUEL

Domestic animals, such as dogs and cats, can enter Mexico with no problem as long as they have recent U.S. health certificates that show their shots are up-to-date. Many new residents have said that immigration officials don't bother to look at the health certificates, but it's good to be on the safe side.

This is a town that overwhelmingly loves animals. Dogs can go pretty much anywhere with their owners. Dogs on rooftops carry on conversations with their fellow animals and with pedestrians on the street below. Large men walk 10-pound poodles. A woman in leopard skin tights parades in the Jardin cuddling her dress-alike Chihuahua, complete with tiny hat.

Stray dogs are an integral part of San Miguel street life, despite valiant efforts of groups that spay and neuter dogs and a dedicated and effective pet adoption agency. The strays by and large look nothing like their counterparts in other parts of the world. Most are not scrawny and they march around seemingly with smiles on their faces and swift trots that resemble investment bankers going off to make their fortunes. They are a joy to watch, particularly in early morning as they keep their appointments for breakfast with friendly residents. The strays must have the skills of public relations tycoons for one frequently hears of adoptions right off the street and the expenditure of sizable sums to de-flea, vaccinate and groom the new best friend. The strays are invariably males; the females don't survive the rigors of life on the street.

Living in San Miguel

Veterinarians

Dr. Edgardo Vazquez Olmos MVZ is the vet of choice for many expats, although his office on upper Mesones is in an area where it's hard to park. He makes house calls. Short-term boarding and grooming. Mesones #5 (facing Academia.) Open 9:00 a.m.-2:00 p.m.; 4:00 p.m.-7:00 p.m.; Saturday, 9:00 a.m.-noon. clinicadeanimales@hotmail.com. **152-6273. 154-8452** for emergencies.

Dr. Robert Merrill Marquez is a highly-regarded vet from Boston. Some pet owners think he is a bit on the expensive side. He makes house calls. Dog grooming and boarding of dogs and cats is also available. Pedro Paramo #67. **152-2901.**

Christina, the vet at SPA, the equivalent of the SPCA, is tireless in her devotion to the SPA animals, even to the point of staying up all night to feed newborn kittens. She is also a large animal veterinarian and she is considered the vet of choice by many horse owners. She can be contacted at SPA. **152-6124.**

Kennels and Grooming

St. Michael's Canine Center offers kennels, dog training and grooming. **Sue Gearhart,** the manager, has a dog park with agility obstacles and other exercise equipment to entertain dogs at her facility in Los Frailes. The walled-in area is open to the public. The vet and dog trainer **Pancho Segura** handle show dogs. Pickup and delivery is available. **154-4182.**

Olimpia Miranda grooms and trains show dogs. Pick-up and delivery. **152-3768.**

Tato & Lore. Open weekdays, 9:00 a.m.-5:00 p.m.; Saturday, 9:00 a.m.-2:00 p.m. Avenida Guadalupe #6. **154-7063.**

Pets

Dog and Puppy Training

Charlotte Peltz conducts classes that focus on problems with behavior and aggression. Diligencias #5. **152-2494.**

Adoption

SPA (Society for the Protection of Animals) is equivalent to the SPCA in the United States. They do a wonderful job placing pets for adoption. Once a week a crew of volunteers comes to the Jardin cuddling puppies and kittens and parading mature dogs. Their success in getting adoptions is impressive. Animals can also be viewed at the SPA clinic. Hours: 10:00 a.m.-2:00 p.m. Calle Los Pinos. **152-6124.**

Bringing Down Your Horse

Horses are considered livestock and they are scrutinized much more carefully than household pets. A full heath certificate, including an active Coggins certificate that certifies the animal is disease-free, is required. If a horse does not have proper certification and proof that appropriate vaccinations have been given, he will be placed in quarantine for a week at the border. Certificates must be dated within two weeks of the planned border crossing. It's important that your U.S. vet is knowledgeable about international regulations.

If you are not bringing your horse in your own trailer, the cost to bring him to San Miguel is between US$3,500 and US$4,000. You'll need a broker in Laredo and then there's the long trek by trailer. Unless you are particularly attached to your horse, you may want to consider buying a horse once you get to San Miguel.

Living in San Miguel

Horseback Riding

Cross-country trailriding in San Miguel can present challenges not present in many parts of the United States. Neighbors are sensitive about crossing property lines and much of the property is fenced. To maintain good relationships with your neighbors it's advisable to negotiate with them about riding on their property.

Horses - Boarding

Most North Americans do not board their horses with Mexicans because they tie the horses and are sometimes casual about putting mares and stallions together.

Rancho La Loma is on the road to Dolores Hidalgo, less than 10 minutes from the light at Calzada de la Estacion. Monthly fee of US$250 includes feed. **152-2121.**

Montecillo Ranch boards horses. The US$175 a month charge includes feed, indoor stall or outdoor covered paddock. Two rings and two outdoor arenas, jumps, riding trails, and tack room. On the road to Dolores Hidalgo, just beyond the Atotonilco turnoff, on the left. Contact Steve DiPiero. **154-5110.**

Physical

PHYSICAL FITNESS
Yoga/Meditation, Pilates, Exercise, Water Aerobics

Yoga

Yoga by Norman is considered by many yoga enthusiasts to have the best yoga in town. Classic yoga poses are the core, interspersed with meditation and spiritually uplifting observations. Walk-ins are welcome. $100 pesos. Classes on weekdays, 10:00 a.m.-11:15 a.m. Meditation Center, just down from Quebrada. E-mail info@yoganorman.com **152-5912** and **152-1852**.

Bellas Artes holds yoga classes on Monday, Wednesday and Friday. Beginners 9:30 a.m.-11:00 a.m.; intermediates 8:00 a.m.-9:30 a.m. H. Macias #75.

Fabienne Gauthier teaches Ashtanga yoga and holds week-long retreats. Yoga classes weekdays at 10:00 a.m.; Thursday at 4:00 p.m. for beginners. Casa Linda at Mesones #101. **154-6137.**

Lydia Wong offers Tai Chi and yoga. Yoga on Monday and Wednesday at 9:30 p.m. Tai Chi classes on Tuesday and Thursday at 9:30 a.m. Casa Linda, Mesones #101. www.lydiawong88.net. **154-4541.**

Meditation

Meditation Center of San Miguel is a serene setting for Buddhist oriented meditation. Sitting and walking

Living in San Miguel

meditation on weekdays, 8:00 a.m. and 8:50 a.m.; Saturday, 10:00 a.m. www.meditationsma.org. Callejon Blanco #4, off Quebrada.

Pilates

Sue Lawrence is a superb Pilates instructor who puts her clients through their paces on the Pilates equipment with patience and humor. Single and 2-person sessions last one hour. $300 pesos. By appointment. **044-415-149-0176**.

Exercise

Santo Domingo Sports Club has a swimming pool that is uncrowded during the day; also weight equipment and stationary bikes that are used for spinning classes. Single class $35 pesos. Office hours: Monday through Thursday, 8:30 a.m.-8:00 p.m.; Friday, 8:30 a.m.-6:00 p.m.; Saturday, 8:30 a.m.-1:00 p.m. Santo Domingo #55. **154-7545**.

En Forma Aerobics Studio specializes in low-impact aerobics. Owner **Linda Cooper** is a long-time resident and personal trainer. Classes on Monday, Wednesday and Friday at 9:30 a.m. $50 pesos per class or $400 pesos by the month. Mesones #14, inside the second courtyard, on the left. **152-0002**.

San Miguel Health and Fitness Center has classes in aerobics, yoga, and Pilates. Also rehabilitation programs for joint replacements and spinal problems. Plaza Pueblito, Stirling Dickinson #28. Open weekdays, 6:00 a.m.-10:00 p.m. Saturday, 8:00 a.m.-3:00 p.m.; Sunday, 9:00 a.m.-1:00 p.m. **154-8395**.

Curves is a 30-minute workout on exercise machines. Ancha de San Antonio #15, Suite C, inside Posada de la Aldea Hotel. **152-8400**.

Physical

Sweat Your Prayers is an idiosyncratic, free-form dance and exercise session with lots of loud, pounding music. You can lie on the floor in silence or dance wildly. Bellas Artes on Sunday, 10:30 a.m.-noon. H. Macias #75.

Feldenkrais Method (Awareness Through Movement) involves highly-concentrated focus on exercising small muscle groups in a subtle, non-violent way. **Paul** is the Feldendrais instructor. Classes are held at Casa Linda, across from the Peralta Theater. Monday and Thursday, 9:00 a.m.-10:00 a.m. Walk-ins are welcome, but arrive on time. $70 pesos. **044-415-151-1603.**

Tai Chi Chuan and **Qigong**
Instituto Allende, 8:00 a.m., Tuesday, Thursday and Saturday. The teacher is **Bob Kaplan**.
044-415-151-7087.

Water Aerobics
Taboada Hot Springs has water aerobics in an Olympic-size pool, with hot springs water. Arrangements can be made for transportation. Classes on Monday, Thursday and Friday, 9:30 a.m.-10:30 a.m. $50 pesos per session or 6 classes for $30 pesos each. Instructor is **Joan Nagle. 152-4821.**

Living in San Miguel

REAL ESTATE

Should I Rent or Buy?

Oldtimers chuckle about the casual first-time tourists who go home after a week having bought homes in San Miguel. Most of these impulse buyers have made substantial gains on their investments. But the past does not necessarily predict the future. The most recent dot.com bubble is a cautionary reminder.

The decision to rent or to buy depends on your pocketbook, your enthusiasm and your intentions. For most newcomers the decision to buy property is based on the lifestyle San Miguel offers. They want to build a life here and their home purchases signal the commitment.

A casual glance at the volume of construction and renovation could lead a newcomer to conclude that this is real estate nirvana. But a conservative investor could make the case that with the enormous amount of building in progress, and with the relatively small base of foreigners, it will take a sizable increase in the foreign population to take up the slack.

Excluding the possibility of capital appreciation, renting makes a good deal of sense. Rents are relatively low and caretaker responsibilities, repairs and maintenance belong to your landlord. You are free and unencumbered. If you rent you may be able to keep your stateside home, or use the capital from its sale and the investment return to maintain your life here.

Living in San Miguel

Rent Now, Perhaps Buy Later?

Most financial advisors would suggest that you rent initially to get the lay of the land, the feeling for neighborhoods, and a sense of how well you like living here. After a few months of renting, you'll know if you want the quiet countryside, the hubbub of Centro or something in between.

Renting is the sensible option if you're low on funds or undecided about your commitment to San Miguel. Your choice of rental properties, in terms of cost and attractiveness, will be widened if you commit to a long-term lease, generally at least 6 months. Rental prices in Centro are higher than in the outlying *colonias*, or neighborhoods. Close to the Jardin a modern, well-furnished one-bedroom with outdoor space will rent for around US$700 a month.

Low-end rentals for one-bedroom apartments start around US$400 a month, long-term, although with persistence and luck small, comfortable units can be found for as little as US$250 a month. If you're on a tight budget be sure to know what's included in the rent; monthly charges for cable, telephone, television, water, gas and electricity can add up.

Since San Miguel has no multiple listing service, the diligent house-hunter is well advised to contact several real estate agents to look over available listings. The weekly *Atencion,* published on Friday, usually has many listings. It's best to be quick on the draw because attractive offerings are snapped up.

Check out the billboards in *bodegas* and small stores all over town. Many property owners post signs on their property offering them for rent.

Real Estate

Can I Afford to Buy?

Property is valued in large measure by its proximity to the Jardin. As a rule, the closer to the Jardin, the more expensive it will be. Properties that are a 7 to 8-minute walk will be over US$250,000; for a 12-minute walk, the range is US$150,000 to US$250,000. Of course, a premium is paid for a quiet street that's not on a bus route. Homes that have extraordinary views, well-planted gardens and are beautifully designed will have premium price tags. Centro has many homes that are priced well over a million dollars.

The pricing exception to the "minutes to the Jardin" rule are the luxurious homes perched on the hillsides east of Centro, in Los Balcones and Atascadero, and the homes above Benito Juarez Park, in Chorro. These no-expense-spared mansions compete with each other for grandeur.

Back to reality. It takes legwork and persistence to find low-priced properties. If you're on a tight budget, with say around US$100,000 for the purchase price, you probably should consider houses away from Centro. Condos in Allende, perhaps a 20-minute walk to the Jardin, can sometimes be purchased for US$120,000. In La Lejona, a 15-minute drive to town, there are many 3-bedroom homes in the US$100,000 range. The area looks rundown, but close by there's a complex of neat condos and more being built.

San Miguel is growing rapidly, Neighborhoods once considered "out-of-town" or less than desirable are now part of mainstream real estate action. The trick, if you're on a limited budget, is to find up-and-coming neighborhoods that over time will become more attractive. Pore over the map of larger San Miguel and walk or drive through neighborhoods such as Allende, Guadalupe, Independencia, and Los Frailes to get the feel of the areas and the distances to Centro. Consider the financial tradeoffs of having to maintain a car, with

Living in San Miguel

the convenience and initial expense of being closer to town.

Often, it's difficult to get a "feel" of a neighborhood because outward appearances are so deceiving. Even in Centro, a walk down Jesus or Umaran might lead you to believe many of the homes are dilapidated. A peek through the door as an owner is entering tells a much different story.

Buying Property

If you *know* you want to spend much of your time here, and you have the funds, buying is probably a sensible choice. You will benefit from any escalation in house prices, real estate taxes are insignificant, and you may be able to find a vacationer to rent your home while you're away. Real estate agents estimate that property appreciation over the last several years has averaged between 12% and 15% a year.

Buying a house is almost always an all-cash transaction, although mortgages will increasingly be part of the real estate scene. Brokers in Texas offer mortgages for up to 25% of the purchase price at interest rates that are 1%-1.5% higher than comparable mortgages in the States. As financing becomes more common it will probably create upward price pressure in the marketplace.

House-hunters typically use more than one real estate agent to get a full understanding of market values and the houses for sale in their price range. Brokers generally share listings but are not required to do so. But there are pitfalls in working with several brokers. Keep close track of the houses you've seen and the brokers who showed them. A buyer who is shown a house by two brokers may have to pay a double commission to complete the purchase.

Real Estate

Property purchases are in many ways a mirror of transactions in the United States, but with some important differences. Joint tenancy, tenants in common and the rights of survivorship are standard. Property purchased in San Miguel will be held in fee simple. But there are important differences in how the transaction is structured. Banks are not involved since mortgages are usually not part of the deal. Banks in the United States, seeking to limit their risk, provide protection to buyers such as accurate appraisals and other documents to ensure the purchase is legitimate. As in the United States, it's important to have an engineer go over the property to be sure there are no surprises. Some buyers who purchased in the dry winter season were not aware of their jeopardy in terms of the possibility of flood damage.

If renovation work seems indicated, contact a contractor to get price estimates on the work *before you make a down payment*. Be sure to check out carefully the contractor's credentials, experience and reputation. Homeowners here are generally happy to recommend contractors with whom they've had good experiences, or your broker can provide recommendations.

When you've found the house of your dreams, the back and forth of offers and counter offers will begin. Typically your broker will act as your representative in transmitting the offers. Be alert for high-pressure tactics. It may be a sign of a shady transaction and even a legitimate broker may not be aware of complications involving the seller. It's not unheard of to have one owner in a joint ownership situation put property on the market without the knowledge of the co-owner. The seller may be anxious to complete the deal before the co-owner is informed. Or, a seller may have a sizable lien on his property and be eager to have a speedy transaction. The lien may be revealed at the closing, but it's often difficult for the buyer to retrieve his deposit, to say nothing of his disappointment. If the

Living in San Miguel

lien is not revealed it may end up being the responsibility of the new owner.

It is crucial to have a local Mexican lawyer involved in the transaction. A local lawyer who represents your interests can save you money and anguish. He knows contract language, and the rules regarding property assessments. Most importantly, he can conduct the research to ensure the transaction is as advertised. It's his duty to protect your interests. *A Mexican lawyer should be engaged before the deposit is handed to the seller or his representative.*

Once an agreement is reached on terms and price, the contract of sale (*compraventa*) will be written in English and Spanish. Upon signing the contract the buyer generally provides a 10% deposit. If the property owner backs out of the deal he is obliged to return an amount that is double the deposit, although getting the premium could mean being tied up in court for years. Some prospective buyers provide more than 10% of the purchase price to discourage a property owner from backing out based on a more favorable offer. Of course, if the buyer fails to complete the transaction, the deposit will usually be forfeited.

At the time the sales contract is signed, or before, a notary public (*notario publico*) will be designated. The notary is a professional who acts on behalf of both the seller and buyer in a neutral role. (San Miguel has 13 *notarios.*) Notaries are appointed governmental officials. As a professional neutral, he has no responsibility to inform you of strategies that could reduce your costs, taxes, assessments or liability.

Notaries manage the paperwork, conduct a title search, record the deed and handle the taxes. Some *notarios* will hold the deposit until the transaction is completed. The property buyer selects the *notario*. Your broker can recommend a notary or you can use one that is

Real Estate

suggested by friends who are experienced in real estate transactions.

If you are not in San Miguel when the house goes into contract, the general practice is to give your broker or lawyer a Power of Attorney (*Poder Notarial*) to represent you at the transaction. If possible, the deposit funds should be held either in your lawyer's hands or in a reputable "third party" account so that if the deal falls through you avoid difficulties in getting the deposit returned. Escrow insurance is available for around U.S. $1,000.

When buying a home be sure the seller has terminated and paid the legally required severance to employees who you do not intend to hire. Severance is based on a formula that includes a Christmas bonus, vacation pay and 20 days' pay for each year of service. A specific form should be completed, signed by the employee and witnessed.

Draw a Mexican Will

Many new homeowners assume that it's sufficient to have their Mexican property included in a stateside will. This is not the case. There are many technicalities concerning the rights of heirs. Unless the will is properly drawn the property could be subject to a punitive 25% transfer tax at the time the property changes ownership. The cost for a will drawn up by your lawyer or *notario* should be around US$200, depending on complications.

Real Estate Lawyers

Compiling a list of recommended lawyers was one of the bigger challenges in writing this book. Residents told horrific stories about lawyers who, once they received their fees, refused to return phone calls or have any contact with the client.

Living in San Miguel

Formal legal proceedings in Mexico are torturous and can take years in the courts before a resolution is reached. Privately negotiated settlements are by far the preferable approach. Listed here are lawyers who have been highly recommended for their professional services.

Reyes Retana is widely considered to be the top lawyer in San Miguel, and also the most expensive. He is skillful in negotiating settlements under difficult circumstances. Retana wrote the code for the State of Guanajuato so he has an encyclopedic knowledge of the laws of this state. Perhaps the legal fees can be reduced a bit by using **Santiago**, an associate in his office. Recreo #5, Altos. **152-3077.**

Eduardo Iglesias is a popular attorney who has been advising clients on real estate purchases for more than a decade. He is also an agent. Aldama #3. **152-6173** or **152-2312.**

Salvador Soto is highly regarded and has been helpful in many real estate transactions. Hospicio #40. **152-0301.**

Clemente Carbajo also comes highly recommended. Recreo #4. **152-1208.**

Goiricelaya Garcia has an excellent reputation for his legal advice and careful research. Across the street from the Biblioteca at Insurgentes #70-A. **152-0063.**

Mexico Advisor has a team of accountants, lawyers and tax experts, knowledgeable about legal and tax issues in both the United States and Mexico. In real estate, as a buyer's representative, they handle escrow, title search, insurance appraisals and estimates. Correo #24. Open weekdays, 9:30 a.m.-7:00 p.m. E-mail: info@mexadv.com. **152-6932** or **152-0586.**

Real Estate

Home Insurance

Many foreign homeowners don't bother to take out home insurance. Most homes are built of brick and concrete, making fire unlikely. But prudent homeowners take out liability protection for injuries to their workers or visitors on their property. A policy from Lloyd's costs around $700 pesos a year.

Construction and Renovation

New construction, or major renovations of a rundown structure, is generally considered to be less costly than the purchase of a home that's ready to occupy. Labor is inexpensive and building costs are considerably less than in the States. Real estate agents estimate that building a *modest* home on a vacant lot will cost around US$45 a square foot; with flourishes, the cost will be US$60 to US$70 a square foot. Thus, a 1,800 square foot house can be built for around US$100,000. Of course, the cost of the land is extra.

If you are buying land from a Mexican family, closing on the land may be delayed while the family clears up problems that may arise over joint ownership of the property. Applications for building permits cannot be submitted until you have the title in hand.

Bids for the cost of construction can follow two lines. As in the United States, the bid can be a detailed list of items to be completed based on a time line for phases of construction. This approach can run up costs every time the owner seeks to change specifications. The alternate approach, which seems to be favored here, is to have bids based on the three phases of construction: the foundation; the completion of the walls; and the final installation of wiring and fixtures. Electrical and metalwork are frequently bid separately. The project manager or contractor will provide the owner with the running costs in terms of the number of crew and hours worked. Since the owner must basically take these

Living in San Miguel

figures on faith, it's important to have confidence in the integrity of the contractor.

If you have extensive building and renovation experience, or fully trust a contractor who has experience in San Miguel, building or a gut renovation is a viable option. Overseeing a building project will probably be more complicated than it would be in the States. Unless you are absolutely fluent in Spanish you won't know how your instructions are being translated by your contractor to the work crew.

Projects generally proceed more casually here; decisions about interior walls, placement of bathrooms and patios are often made as the work progresses. Since building in San Miguel is a "fluid" process in which plans evolve on an almost daily basis, several residents feel it's important to have a hands-on presence as construction proceeds.

Building Permits

In Centro (an area of about 7 square blocks from the Parroquia), building and renovation presents its own set of challenges. Rigid restrictions apply regarding facades and windows. Plans must be approved by the local planning authorities, who will cast eagle eyes on your plans. There are differing views as to whether revisions to an approved plan should be submitted to the city authorities. Some home builders just move along, prepared to pay the penalties if discovered; others comply because they don't want the hassle. Many newcomers go through the permit revision process because they believe that as guests in the community they are obliged to play by the rules.

INAH (Institute of Anthropology and History) is the city's permitting agency in the historic district. After approvals are received from the city, the plans go to Guanajuato where they are reviewed by federal

Real Estate

authorities. Depending on the scope of the project and your architect's or project manager's relationship with the planning agencies, the process can take as little as a week, or as long as 5 months. Often the submission of the plans to the authorities is held up by delays in receiving the deed. Several residents complained that they were ready with the plans, but the deed wasn't given over. No demolition or new construction is allowed before the permits are received.

When the permit is in place, they owner must have a *Bitacora de Obra*, a log book that is used by the project manager to record work progress on a weekly basis. This log book is the record the government official or inspector uses on visits to the project. Visits can be as frequent as once a week.

Generally the project manager pays the work crew by the week. Many residents bring the pesos to the manager in front of the work crew so they know the *jefe* is not skimming money that should be used for wages. The project manager is expected to submit to the owner on a weekly basis an itemized list of the cost of labor and materials.

Unanticipated glitches can arise. One new owner wanted a written agreement from the project manager that the work crew was being hired by the manager, not by the owner, so that the manager would be responsible for paying social security and for personal liability. This was a deal breaker, until the owner backed down. First, the manager and his crew viewed themselves as equals and if one signed they should all sign and the crew refused. Workers are averse to social security, probably because working off the books is more profitable. Another factor is that Mexico's long history of enslavement taught them that individual dignity and respect are all important. The notion of a written agreement smacked to them of distrust.

Living in San Miguel

Property owners who are building or remodeling should be aware of the importance of contractors paying payroll taxes on the wages of construction workers. If the taxes aren't paid or the payroll is not handled properly, home owners can be assessed the taxes, with fines and interest. Property owners should confirm that taxes are being paid by seeing the actual returns and paid receipts.

The recent experience of several residents is that cost estimates for construction are invariably on the low side. A reserve fund of between 30% and 40% of the initial construction budget should be set aside to cover unexpected costs. "You never know what's behind a wall," is the way one new owner put it. Then too, it may turn out that the specified molding or stair brace is unavailable and an alternate approach is required. And as construction progresses, owners add items that had not been thought about in the design stage.

Of course, just as in the States, horror stories about renovation disasters regularly make the rounds. Often these disasters can be traced to a *failure to fully check out the credentials and experience of the architect or engineer who prepares the plans, and/or a failure to fully check out the credentials and experience of the contractor or project manager.* The best protection for assuring an expedited, well-managed project is to engage an architect or contractor who has lengthy experience is gaining permit approvals and successfully completing projects.

Architects and Contractors

Architects in San Miguel do more than create design plans; they take the plans through the city approval process, suggest contractors and oversee construction. The service is vital because of language difficulties and the fact that most new residents are unfamiliar with the way approvals and construction move forward in San Miguel.

Real Estate

Construction is generally concrete; dry wall is not used in Mexico. Insulation can be a problem. Some contractors put ground-up lava in the concrete mix to buffer noise in Centro and to help insulate the structure.

Patricia Merrill Marguez is not only an architect, but also a real estate broker, builder and owner of a bed & breakfast. She's highly professional and considered a joy to work with. She suggests contractors who oversee the work crews. **152-4553** and **044-415-151-0227.**

Nicole Bisgaard comes highly recommended. By background she's Danish, Mexican and American. She's skillful in creating beautiful spaces that involve extensive renovations. **152-0243.**

Estela de Lucia is a highly-regarded young architect from Uruguay. She sparks with ideas and is inventive in coming up with solutions that work within a budget. Prolong. Cinco de Mayo #6. estela@intrading.net. **154-5480.**

Gerardo Lopez Salas is a contractor who is considered reliable, responsive and a good value. His English is limited. His clients have used Evaresto Garcia Jimenez (**044-415-101-4511**.) for translation.
044-415-153-2231. controldebrasma@yahoo.com.mx.

Javier Garay Lopez is a local engineer and general contractor who supervises construction. He has an excellent reputation and is considered to be congenial to work with. **044-415-103-3275.**

Juan Macias has an excellent reputation as a contractor and manager of work crews. His clients are extremely satisfied with his careful attention to detail. **150-0148.**

Useful Books
For a prospective renovator who is not fluent in Spanish, several books can help bridge the language gap between

Living in San Miguel

the owner and the construction crew. The books are all available on Amazon.com.

> *McGraw-Hill Constructionary. English-Spanish Construction Dictionary.* International Conference of Building Officials (ICBO);
> *Construction Spanish*, A.P. Scott;
> *Easy Spanish for Construction*, by Hamilton Mitchell.

Property Managers

Property managers serve a variety of functions, depending on the owner's needs and his pocketbook. For large properties they can hire, oversee and pay the staff and take care of all facets of keeping the property in tip-top shape. For more modest properties, the manager may arrange for renters when the owner is away. The costs for these services depend on circumstances. The major real estate firms provide property management services. There are also independent contractors who offer this service.

Evaresto Garcia Jimenez, known by everyone as Evaresto, is a seasoned property and rental manager. He is also a font of knowledge and good sense. He has a wealth of experience at his fingertips, not just about real estate. He can recommend a computer expert, suggest a plumber, or help you buy a car in Queretaro. He's friendly, available and a true San Miguel treasure. His email is evaristogj@yahool.cmmx.
044-415-101-4511.

Renting Your Home to Vacationers

San Miguel has two distinct rental seasons: the snowbirds in December, January, February and March; and southerners, predominatly Texans escaping the humidity and heat in June, July and August. These are the months you'll be most likely to find a tenant.

Real Estate

Houses close to the Jardin are the most popular, and listings usually include this distance in minutes to walk there. A recent review of listings on the Internet found few vacation offerings below US$2,000 a month.

To legally rent your property you should file with **Hacienda** *(Secretaria de Hacienda y Credito Publico)*, the Mexican government equivalent of the I.R.S. As a rule taxes due on a rental are around 8% of the gross rent.

Most residents who rent their properties for a short time do not file. But recently *Hacienda* has become more vigilant in seeking out tax evaders, even going so far as to monitor Web site offerings and contacting property owners who are looking for tenants. *Hacienda* is at Mesones #71, on the ground floor. Open weekdays, 8:00 a.m.-3:00 p.m. **152-0037.**

Some owners engage property managers to rent their homes; others use the Internet to list their properties. Some join home exchange services, generally over the Internet, to trade time in their homes for homes in areas they want to visit.

Using the Internet
Many residents have had success renting their homes through the Internet. The Internet sites direct you through the listing procedure. Here are a few popular sites:
        www.vrbo.com
        www.vacation-homes-sanmiguel.com
        www.san-miguel-house-rentals.com

Living in San Miguel

RESTAURANTS AND CATERING

Dining out in San Miguel is a major activity. There are dozens of restaurants of every variety and price range. Several guidebooks give a complete roster of restaurants. Listed here are among residents' favorites.

L'Invito presents classic Italian fare on the terrace inside the Instituto Allende, to the left of the entrance. Proprietor Silvia Bernardini is ever watchful and an engaging conversationalist who proudly suggests mouth-watering specialties from her kitchen. Views of the town from the terrace are spectacular. Open every day, 1:00 p.m.-midnight. Ancha de San Antonio #20. **152-7333.**

Mama Mia features a lively, friendly bar and a full menu of Mexican favorites. This is a favorite hangout for locals. Open 8:00 a.m.-3:00 a.m. Umaran #8. **152-2063**.

Tio Lucas is known for its steaks. The atmosphere is festive, with live jazz every evening. The bar is a popular gathering spot, particularly on Monday nights. Open noon to midnight every day. Mesones #103. **152-4996.**

Hotel Sautto is known for its succulent mussels and other Italian seafood specialties. The service tends to be lethargic. Large and gracious patio. H. Macias #59. **152-0051.**

Nirvana Restaurant-Fusion is the top choice for many residents. Menu features distinctive flavors based on a blending of world cuisines, East and West. H. Macias #56-A. **150-0067.**

El Bacha offers a break from Mexican cuisine. Middle Eastern specialties are featured from the buffet or *a la carte.* The broad terrace offers dining at widely separated tables that have commanding views of San Miguel. Calle Piedras Chinas #21. **152-4339.**

Hacienda Los Laureles features gracious courtyard dining. Surrounding the courtyard are small shops, including one that has spectacular Mexican Indian pottery. The courtyard is a favorite hangout for late afternoon socializing. Open 1:00p.m.-10:00 p.m., except on Tuesday. Hidalgo #4. **152-4212.**

For less formal dining, with modest prices, try:
La Palapa which is known for its fish tacos and a tasty sauce made from a secret recipe. At $10 pesos apiece this is probably the best food bargain in town. Hamburgers, and chili dogs and a fabulously rich carrot cake are also on the menu. Morris and Ray are the friendly hosts who make everyone feel at home. Calle Nueva #8, under the big yellow "Sol" beer tent. Open Monday through Saturday, noon-6:00 p.m.

La Grotta specializes in thin-crust pizza and Italian cuisine. Cuadrante #5. **152-4119.**

El Buen Café is a friendly neighborhood gathering spot; fine for morning coffee and snacks. Delicious baked goods to-go. Open Monday through Saturday, 9:00 a.m.-8:00 p.m. Jesus #23. **152-5807.**

Café de la Parroquia has delicious luncheon specialties and is popular for Sunday brunch. Open air dining in a delightful patio. To the left of the patio is El Tecolote, the best bookstore in town. Open Tuesday through Saturday, 7:30 a.m.-4:00 p.m.; Sunday, 7:30 a.m.-2:00 p.m. Jesus #11. **152-3161.**

Restaurants

Hecho en Mexico offers friendly courtyard dining and huge, tasty Caesar salads. Enchiladas are a standout speciality. Ancha de San Antonio #8. Open daily, noon-10:00 p.m. **154-6383.**

Casa Don Quixote features *arrachera* beef that is marinated in a distinctive Mexican sauce. Grilled and barbecued meats are served on a gracious terrace. Margaritas are the biggest in town. Open 1:00 p.m.-10:00 p.m. Closed on Sunday. Prolongacion de Pila Seca #55, at the far end of Pila Seca. **152-0807.**

Restaurant Lila is a tiny, new spot that offers Italian specialties and desserts. If you stop by for morning cappuccino try the airy fried pastry rings covered with powered sugar. Open 10:00 a.m.-9:00 p.m. Closed on Tuesday. Terraplen #2-C. **044-415-101-3393.**

Nutri Verdi is a vegetarian restaurant that uses the freshest vegetables and other healthy ingredients. Dine indoors or on a small outdoor patio. Cuna de Allende #17.

Casa Colon offers a delicious *comida* of soup, Mexican special entrees and coffee for $45 pesos. Mesones #25, 5 doors down from the Civic Plaza.

Catering

Let's throw a party – a housewarming or sundowners' celebration. Cooking too big a deal? Just a few calls and an hour or so of preparation and you'll have a hit!

La Europea for booze. They deliver from Canal #13. Closed on Sunday. **152-2003.**

La Cava is a deli that has a tantalizing assortment of imported cheeses and Italian meats. Open weekdays, 10:30 a.m.-3:00 p.m.; 5:30 p.m.- 8:30 p.m. Zacateros #40, close to the beginning of Ancha de San Antonio.

Living in San Miguel

La Colmena, called the "Blue Door", has *empanadas* - small pies filled with tuna, cheese or chorizo. Reloj #21. **152-1422**.

BBQ Bob's features shish-ka-Bob's of pork, chicken and beef. They are juicy and pre-cooked so all that's needed is to heat them up. Open every day but Sunday, 10:00 a.m.-5:00 p.m. Salida de Celaya #6. **152-8983**.

Harry's Market for fresh shellfish, seafood and gourmet specialties. Hildago #10. Open Monday through Saturday, 10:00 a.m.-6:00 p.m.; Sunday, 10:00 a.m.-2:00 p.m. **152-3838**.

La Buena Vida for crusty home-made bread and tantalizing pastries prepared in the classic French tradition. Open Monday through Saturday, 8:00 a.m.-5:00 p.m. H. Macias #72. **152-2211**.

Sensual Chocolatiers can add the final touch to your feast. The chocolate is the highest caliber and irresistible. Located inside the El Palacio China (China Palace) courtyard, on the left. Mesones #57. **154-6947**.

As an added touch, you may want to engage **Trio Amigos** to entertain your guests with traditional Mexican music. Juan, Fidel and Jacinto provide lively and romantic ballads. Contact Juan at **154-9386**.

El Buen Café's Kris Rudolph is a fabulous caterer who produces outstanding food for large parties and weddings. This is really a rare skill; she handles all unforeseen problems with calm and grace. Contact her at the restaurant. Jesus #23. **152-5807**.

Night Kitchen Caterers's Michele Vallon has 25 years' experience catering New York City corporate affairs and private parties. Her cuisine is international and each party is styled to give a special look and taste. Fabulous presentations. Also cocktails, buffets, and hors d'oeuvers to-go. **152-3099**.

SERVICE CLUBS

Rotary Club meets on Wednesday at 8:00 p.m. at the Posada de la Aldea, Ancha San Antonio #9.

Lions Club International meets the 1st and 3rd Thursdays for lunch at 1:00 p.m. Don Quixote restaurant, Prolongacion de Pila Seca #35.

SUPPORT GROUPS

Cancer Support Group meets the first Monday of the month, at the home of Alexandra Norton, Loreto #11, Casita #10, from 5:00 p.m.-7:00 p.m.
152-5366.

Alcoholics Anonymous – 12 Steps holds 23 meetings a week, every day. Meeting times are listed weekly in *Atencion*. 20 de Enero Norte #10, Room E., Col. San Antonio. **152-5110**.

Living in San Miguel

Spanish

SPANISH Ð LEARN IT!

This is the single most important thing you can do to make your life in San Miguel a success.

The joy of being able to converse with Mexicans, who welcome all attempts to speak their language, however primitive, is unbounded. Of course, Americans have lived here for years with only the most rudimentary phrases, and you can too. But to experience the richness of the culture and the joys and sorrows of your Mexican friends, Spanish is a must. It will enrich your life and make everyday contacts more meaningful. You can listen in on conversations, joke with fruit vendors, appreciate the words of Spanish songs, and celebrate with your neighbors, and most important, be able to give directions to your maid. San Miguel is blessed with a wide variety of Spanish language classes. To experience life to the full in this colonial town, you must be able to speak its language. And increasing your mastery can be a continuing pleasure.

Warren Hardy Spanish is considered by many to be the relatively painless way to learn to speak the language. Classes provide the grammatical basics for developing conversational skills. His fast-paced approach pairs students in exercises, and uses a team of trained local professionals to aid the learning process. The school also provides tutors in the Warren Hardy method for independent study. www.warenhardy.com San Rafael #6. **152-4728**.

Living in San Miguel

Academia Hispano Americana offers total immersion programs for all levels, and an accredited diploma program in Spanish as a second language. Mesones #4. www.ahaspeakspanish.com. **152-0349** and **152-4349.**

Instituto Allende has a wide range of instruction at all levels and program lengths. Ancha de San Antonio #20. www.instituto-allende.edu.mx **152-0190.**

Instituto de Habla Hispana. Offers one-week classes to four-week sessions. Calzada de la Luz #25. www.mexicospanish.com **152-0713.**

Spanish Through Cinema. Professional linguist and translator **Bassia Bar-Chai** uses films to help students with pronunciation and comprehension. **154-9239.** dbbarchai@yahoo.com

Destinos uses a 52-episode *telenovela* produced by PBS to hone conversational skills. 5:00 p.m. on Wednesday at the Biblioteca. Kendal Dodge Butler. **044-415-103-2312.**

Lilia Trapaga comes highly recommended as a Spanish tutor. Lilux80@hotmail.com. **154-5376.**

SPORTS

Golf

Malanquin Country Club is a 9-hole course. Green fees are $456 pesos; caddy, $80 pesos; electric cart, $156 pesos. Non-members must tee-off after 1:00 p.m. on weekends. The facility also has a driving range, swimming pool and 4 clay tennis courts. On the road to Celaya, a short distance south of town. Open Tuesday through Sunday, 9:00 a.m.-9:00 p.m. **152-0516** or **154-8210**.

Hotel El Santuario Spa & Golf has a 9-hole, par 3 course. Green fees are $300 pesos; golf cart $200 pesos. On the road to Dolores Hidalgo, about 15 minutes from town. **152-0335**.

Coming Soon: The **Jack Nicklaus Golf Course** on the road to Dolores Hidalgo. Jack Nicklaus is on the board of the development and will be a member of the club. It is being financed by U.S. investors. The new country club community known as **Las Puertas** will have villas and estates.

Tennis

Walter Weber's has 3 clay courts and is popular with residents. The cost is $60 pesos an hour. Callejon de San Antonio #12. For reservations call **152-0659**.

Hotel d' Minas has drop-in drill sessions for doubles and singles every morning except Sunday. No need to

Living in San Miguel

register, just show up. The cost is $100 pesos for 1° hours of play. Private lessons and hitting sessions must be booked in advance. Contact Alan Mack at: **044-415-103-3246** or **154-4334.**

Malanquin Country Club (see "Golf" above) One-day tennis guest memberships available.
152-0516 or **154-8210.**

Hotel Posada de la Aldea has 2 tennis courts and 3 pros, headed by Mauricio Chauvet. Lessons given on most mornings; children's programs in the afternoon. Cost is $100 pesos for 1° hours of play. Ancha de San Antonio #15. **154-5179.**

Candelaria Racquet Club offers vacation and long-term memberships. They have clay courts and a gym. On the road to Dolores Hidalgo, 6 km from town. Elisa Garcia. **044-415-153-8795.**

Bird Walks

The Audubon Society conducts bird walks the third Sunday of every month, starting at the Instituto at 8:00 a.m. Donation of $100 pesos is requested from non-members. A hat and binoculars are recommended. For information call Fen at
044-415-153-5438.

Sports Equipment and Rentals

Deportes Aces sells sports balls of all kinds; soccer, volleyballs, basketballs, sports gloves and shoes, team sport jerseys, trophies and other sports paraphernalia. H. Macias #43. No telephone.

Sol Y Luna rents bicycles, motor scooters and 4-wheelers. Also conducts hiking and camping trips. www.solylunatours.com. Correo #41 and Hospicio #10. **154-8599.**

TAX PREPARATION

If you are out of the United States at tax time you are entitled to a 2-month extension in filing the return and paying federal taxes. You are considered "out of the country" if you live outside the United States. For more information, check the I.R.S. Web site at www.irs.com.

Raoul Rodriguez at **Mexican Advisor** is a financial planner who also prepares tax returns. Correo #24. **152-0586.**

Melanie Nance had been preparing tax returns in San Miguel for many years. Reloj #45. **154-9230.** mnance@unisono.net.mx.

Andrew Barker is a U.S. trained CPA and lawyer who works out of Mexico City and is highly recommended in the fields of tax returns, accounting and investment planning. He works with clients by e-mail. andrewmbarker@yahoo.com.

Josefina R. de Angel is a bilingual accountant with many clients here. Palma #9. jrtangel@hotmail.com **152-2119** and **152-2089.**

Sergio Hernandez is also recommended by residents. **152-1350.**

Living in San Miguel

TRANSPORTATION and TOURS

Airport Connections

Aside from services provided by travel agencies, many private car services offer rides to the airports. Some of these car services are not reliable so be sure to check out their track records with friends.

Leon International Airport

Viajes de San Miguel has scheduled, reliable, 24-hour shuttle service, for US$27 per person. Credit cards accepted. Open weekdays, 9:00 a.m.-7:00 p.m.; Saturday, 10:00 a.m.-2:00 p.m. Reservations can be made on the Internet; confirmations via e-mail take awhile. www.viajessanmiguel.com. Sollano #4. **152-2537.**

Turisticos Rodriguez also offers regularly scheduled shuttle service to Leon for US$25. Open weekdays, 10:00 a.m.-7:00 p.m.; Saturday,10:00 a.m.-2:00 p.m., and on the net www.airportdriversma.com. Hidalgo #8 int. #4. **154-6168.**

Ritchie Granados is a reliable, bilingual driver who provides a shuttle service to the Leon airport. He will take you to meet your visitors for no extra charge. **044-415-153-5576.**

Mexico City Airport
Viajes de San Miguel also has regular shuttle service to the Mexico City airport for US$50 per person.

Living in San Miguel

Reservations can also be made for your return to San Miguel. (See above for reservations.)

Turisticos Rodriguez offers comparable service to and from the Mexico City airport for US$50 per person. (See above for reservations.)

Local Public Transportation

Buses
Public buses are a bargain at $4 pesos. The mayor is working with the independent bus companies to encourage them to purchase new, smaller, less-polluting vehicles.

Buses to the close-in communities leave about every 15 minutes; buses traveling further out are generally on a half-hour schedule. Intra-town buses leave from the Civic Plaza.

Top of the Plaza on Colegio. Buses to Gigante, La Luz, Jardines, Valle, Cereso and Ignacio Ramirez.

Bottom of the Plaza, on Insurgentes. Buses to the Central Bus Station (*Estacion Central*), San Felipe, Santa Julia, Malanquin, San Luis Rey, Allende and Jardines II, Nigromante, and San Antonio.

Taxis
Taxis are inexpensive. You can pick them up on the street or at the taxi stand at the northeast corner of the Jardin, at Relox.

If you call a cab the charge will include round-trip for the driver, but the ride is a bargain, usually no more than $30 pesos. Ask in advance for the charge. Drivers do not expect tips. **Radio Taxi: 152-4501.**

At first, you may want to ask the driver the cost of the ride to a particular location. It doesn't take long to get

Transportation and Tours

the sense of the fare. A trip with grocery bags down from Gigante is $20 pesos to Centro. Longer rides are $30 pesos.

For a trip to Escondido or La Gruta hot springs, ask the fare in advance and perhaps request that the driver pick you up at a pre-determined time. It usually works. If not, buses on the road to Dolores Hidalgo run frequently, or you can hitch a ride from a visitor at the hot springs who's returning to San Miguel.

Buses to Points Outside San Miguel

Buses leave from the main bus terminal on Calzada de la Estacion, the extension of Canal. Deluxe luxury buses are the most comfortable; they have bathrooms and movies. First class buses have bathrooms. Second class buses have no bathrooms and often make many stops along the route.

ETN, Deluxe Luxury to Mexico City, Queretaro. **152-6407**

Primera Plus, First Class Mexico City, Queretaro, Guanajuato, Leon and Guadalajara. **152-7323**

Primera Plus, Second Class. Guanjuato, Leon, Guadalajara. **152-7323.**

Flecha Amarilla Second Class Mexico City, Queretaro, Guanajuato, Dolores Hidalgo, San Luis Potosi, Celaya. **152-5043**

Pegasso Plus First Class Mexico City, Queretaro. **152-0725**

Herradura de Plata Second Class Mexico City, Queretaro, Dolores Hidalgo. **152-0725**

Living in San Miguel

Omnibus de Mexico First Class. Guanajuato. **152-3218**

Transportes Del Norte First Class Monterrey, Laredo, TX. **152-2237**

Americanos Laredo, San Antonio, Dallas, Houston, Atlanta. **152-2237**

Travel Agencies

Viajes de San Miguel
Tickets for international and domestic flights. Also conducts tours to colonial cities and has a shuttle service to the airports. Accepts major credit cards. Open weekdays, 9:00 a.m.-2:30 p.m.; 4:30 p.m.-7:00 p.m.; Saturday 10:00 a.m.-2:00 p.m. Sollano #4 (inside the courtyard.) Reservations on the Internet at www.viajessanmiguel.com. **152-2832** and **152-2537.**

Viajes Vertiz
American Express travel services, cruises and air tickets. Airport shuttle. Hidalgo #1-A.
152-186 and **152-0499**.

Tours

In and around San Miguel
Historic Walking Tour
Groups gather in the Jardin, across from the Parroquia at 9:45 a.m. on Wednesday and Friday. The 2-hour tour is on level terrain. $100 peso contribution to Patronato Pro Ninos, which provides medical care for under-privileged children.

House & Garden Tour
This venerable institution brings the community and visitors together on Sundays at the Biblioteca, at noon. Starting at 11:00 a.m., costumed musicians play in the courtyard creating a festive atmosphere. Off-duty public buses provide the transport from house to house. The

Transportation and Tours

tour usually features three homes. The $150 peso contribution benefits the Biblioteca educational charity.

Saturday Adventure Tours
Tours visit out-of-town sites such ranches, haciendas, vineyards and monasteries. Weekly flyers give the locations to be visited. The cost is $150 pesos. Tickets are available at El Pegaso and Casa Maxwell and in the Jardin on Friday mornings and on Saturday before the 10:30 a.m. departure. The money benefits El Centro de Crecimiento, the school for handicapped children.

Out of Town

The Lions Club offers overnight tours to sites and towns of historical interest. A portion of the tour cost is donated to the club's program that supplies eyeglasses to the needy. The tours are extremely well run and are usually sold out shortly after being announced. **152-0934.**

San Miguel Travel (Jenna Oliver and **Jerry Hunt)** conducts specialized tours to many of the outlying towns and villages. Tours can be arranged to accommodate specific interests. Highly personalized service. www.sanmigueltravel.com. **044-415-103-8887.**

Teocalli specializes in tours to the colonial towns in central Mexico. They are led by bilingual guide **Paul Guerin**. Refugio Norte 4, Col. San Antonio.
154-7339.

PMC (Promotion of Mexican Culture) conducts field trips to artisans' workshops, nature tours and visits to archaeological sites, day trips and overnight. Hidalgo #18. **152-0121**, and **154-5312.**

Living in San Miguel

Volunteers

VOLUNTEER and DONATION OPPORTUNITIES

Hundreds of opportunities exist to apply your energy, skills and financial resources to help the needy. By volunteering you'll have the satisfaction of being useful; and it's a good way to meet like-minded people. The groups listed here are only a fraction of the nearly limitless possibilities. *Amigos* is an intermittent publication that features worthy projects and includes a directory of groups that need your volunteer help and contributions. To receive a copy email: sudhir@amembalandassociates.com.

Casa Hogar Don Bosco is a live-in center for teenage girls that provides education and support for adolescents who are no longer able to live at home. Three dedicated nuns run the facility for 30 girls with no support from the government or the church. Sollano #14. Contact Sally Reid, at **152-8678.**

Mujeres en Cambio (Women in Change) provides scholarships (for books, transportation and uniforms) so that girls from the countryside around San Miguel can continue their schooling beyond the early grades. Some 150 girls from 10 rural communities are receiving scholarships; some of them now attend universities and advanced technical schools. Contact Marjorie Zap at sapster@unisono.net.mx.

Santuario Hogar Guadalupano Mexiquito, an orphanage for boys, seeks US $20,000 to renovate its rundown facilities: the orphanage has no heat, kitchen and bathrooms are in poor condition. Tax-deductible

Living in San Miguel

donations can be made at **Border Crossings**, Calle Correo #19.

Centro de Crecimiento provides physical therapy, including swimming pool exercises, academic classes in primary grades, and arts and crafts for handicapped children. Volunteers help with the children. This professionally-run program has existed for more than 20 years. Zamora Rios 6-C. **152-0318.**

Feed the Hungry provides more than 3,000 nutritious hot meals a day to needy children at 15 locations in and around San Miguel. It's sponsored by St. Paul's Church. Correo #19. **152-2402.** E-mail: contact@feedthehungrysma.org.

Mujeres Productoras is a co-op that helps women in outlying areas to produce and market their handicrafts –baskets, clothing and home furnishings. Many of the women are heads of households; their husbands and sons have migrated to the United States for employment. Recently, Mujeres Productoras opened a store in San Miguel to sell their wares. The store, *Ya Tsedi Behna* (The Power of Women, in the indigenous Otomi language) is in the courtyard at Mesones #38, in front of the Civic Plaza.

SPA (*Sociedad Protectora de Animales*) is a pet adoption clinic, the SPCA of San Miguel. SPA always needs dog walkers and pet lovers to brush and give affection to the animals. The organization is run on a shoe string and is struggling to survive. Visit the animals or volunteer from noon to 2:00 p.m. Los Pinos #7, a right turn off Calzada de la Estacion, just before the bus station. **152-6124**, or **154-5930**.

Amigos de Animales provides free sterilizations and has a mobile clinic. Donations can be left at **La Conexion**, Box 139A, Aldama #3. E-mail: sudhir@amembalandassociates.com. **152-1028.**

Volunteers

ALMA provides care for senior citizens, including shelter for street people, the lost and confused. Donations can be dropped off at **La Conexion**, Mailbox 5K, Aldama #3. Tax-deductible checks should be made payable to the San Miguel Educational Foundation, Attention ALMA. Calle Jacaranda, La Lejona. **152-7210.**

Biblioteca Adopt-a-Shelf is looking for volunteers to work 2-hours a week, you choose the time. For training sessions, see Anna Buchanan in the Biblioteca Patio.

Radio NPR, A.C. is a new project pioneered by Bob Ellison. He's in the process of getting the first Mexican license to transmit this Stateside channel into San Miguel. He needs help in compiling a computerized list of prospective members of the new station. **152-1365.**

Living in San Miguel

Books and Websites

WEB SITES AND BOOKS ABOUT SAN MIGUEL

Four San Miguel Web sites provide a wealth of information about life in San Miguel, including calendars of events, the arts, and, of course, extensive real estate listings.

www.portalsanmiguel.com
www.sanmiguelguide.com
www.internetsanmiguel.com
www.thesanmiguelchronicles.com

For information about local government and projects around town try www.sanmiguelallende.gob.mx The English language version is under construction.

For answers to specific questions about living in San Miguel, go to:
www.coollist.com, a general list server that has two e-mail addresses that put you in touch with residents. On Google go to the Web site and look for "civilsma" or "sma." It's easy to join the list and it's free. "Sma" is full of political screed; "civilsma" is, as it suggests, more civilized.

There's no shortage of books about San Miguel.

The Insider's Guide to San Miguel (14th edition, 2004) by Archie Dean is the most popular and useful guide to all things San Miguel.

Living in San Miguel

Our Caring Community: Your Resources in San Miguel de Allende, is an indispensable booklet and resource for all matters that have to do with the practical aspects of medical care, be it doctors who make house calls, the availability of nursing care, medical equipment, services for the homebound or pharmacies, restaurants, and laundries that deliver. It's an impressive resource that should be a model for this type of information in other communities. Available at the Biblioteca and other bookstores, or through the publisher, Marge Zap, at her e-mail address: mzapster@unisono.net.mx.

The Best of San Miguel, by Joseph Harmes, is a chatty, well-researched recent book (2004) that has fascinating anecdotal information as well as suggestions. The book is particularly strong on bars and restaurants.

On Mexican Time by Tony Cohan, is an affectionate account of a writer and an artist who relocated to San Miguel. (paperback US$10 on Amazon.com.)

Nothing to Declare: Memoirs of a Woman Traveling Alone, by Mary Morris ($10 on Amazon.com.)

Live Well in Mexico: How to Relocate, Retire and Increase Your Standard of Living, by Ken Luboff (US$11 on Amazon.com.)

A Gringo Guide to Living in San Miguel, William J. Conaway (US$10) www.mexicocolonial.com

Walking Mexico's Colonial Heartland, William J. Conaway (US$15) www.mexicocolonial.com

A Gringo Guide to a Mexican Kitchen, William J. Conaway (US$22.50) www.mexicocolonial.com

Also helpful is the telephone directory, *JuARde 2005*, as in "who are they," which can be purchased at the Casa de Papel, Biblioteca and other outlets.

ACKNOWLEDGEMENTS

So many residents and visitors contributed to this book that it's impossible to acknowledge them all. For months I pounded the cobblestones, reporter's notebook in hand, ready for any snippet a friend, acquaintance or resident would bring my way. The expat community is generous. And so they were to me, going out of their way to mention new found pleasures and resources.

I can single out only a few residents who were particularly generous with their time and thoughtful advice. To Jim Bolen for his experience owning a car in San Miguel; to Marty Lieberman for his insistence that we remind newcomers of the benefits of adopting a casual, *no problema* approach to the Mexican lifestyle; to Ruth Hyba, the proprietor of La Mansion del Bosque, for her sage advice and providing a breakfast spot for the author to gain insights, along with a good meal; to Marge Zap for the resources she uncovered for the booklet *Our Caring Community*; to Ana Glazener and Susan Sargeant who contributed importantly to the section on schools and kids' activities.

Christopher Finkelstein in the Mayor's office was generous with his time in explaining facets of San Miguel life that were unclear to me.

Cynthia Greenawalt took me on excursions to look at many rural communities and explained to me the ins and outs of owning a horse.

Living in San Miguel

Miguel Montemayor at Casa de Papel was more than generous in his encouragement of this venture, suggesting contacts and answering a seemingly unending number of questions.

Meryl Musgrave and members of www.coollist.com are owed a big debt of thanks. This is the Internet at its best, members of the San Miguel community in dialogue asking each other for recommendations for everything from car mechanics to podiatrists. It is a treasure trove of information and I encourage other residents to join the fun.

Luba' eagle eyes and her strong editorial abilities helped bring clarity to my copy. Her suggestions on format and technical details immensely improved the book.

Curt Hahn very generously provided the gorgeous cover photograph, and cover design for the book. He and his wife Cele were unstinting in their encouragement of this venture.

No publishing endeavor is done alone. I'm particularly indebted to William J. Conaway for his advise and tangible assistance. He sheparded the book through its earliest stages, secured a printing house, worked meticulously through the intricacies of layout and offered suggestions that only a long-term resident can provide. His gentle guiding hand is reflected throughout.

Finally, my warm thanks to Claire Francy, in Lake Worth, Florida for her encouragement, constructive criticism and help with organizing the material.

Thank you all. I hope *Living in San Miguel* will make it easier for newcomers to quickly and happily adapt to this unique and wonderful community.

Index

A

A Gringo Guide to Living in San Miguel 166
ABCD 92
Abraham Campos Ortega 49, 76
Academia Hispano Americana 150
accountant 153
accounting 153
Acting 31
acupuncturist 105
after school basketball 91
after-school life 90
Alcoholics Anonymous 147
Alexa Fullerton 74
Alfonso Alarcon 66
Allende 40
ALMA 163
American Consulate 59
Americanos 158
Amigos 161
Amigos de Animales 162
Anado McLaughlin 66
Andrew Barker 153
Ann Bowles 116
Anne-Marie Midy 81
Antigua Case Canela 80
AOL access 53
Appliance Repairs 77
Appliances 77
Araiz – Punto com 56
Architects 138
Ashtanga yoga 123
Atabal 89
Atascadero 41
Atencion 29, 111, 128, 147
ATM machines 21
audiologist 105
Audubon Society, The 152
Aurora 41
Authors' Sala 36
auto insurance 18
automatic withdrawal 12
Azteca 41
Azulejos Talavera Cortes 77

B

Backgammon 30
bakeries 61
Bambu Day Spa 115
Banamex 22
Banca Serfin 22
Bancomer 22
Bandala 117
bank accounts online 12
Banorte 22
barrios 39
Baseball for kids 91
basic photography 35
Bassia Bar-Chai 150
Bazar Romero & Flores 79
BBQ Bob's 146
Bellas Artes 31, 34, 123
Belly dancing 35
Bibiana Mora Orvananos 113
Biblioteca 92
Biblioteca Adopt-a-Shelf 163
Biblioteca Giftshop 27
Biblioteca's Computer Center 56
bicultural experience 88
bicycle rental 152
Bill Lieberman 35
Bitacora de Obra 137
Block Busters 111
boarding horses 122
Bob Kaplan 125
body treatments 115
bodywork 16
Bonanza 62
Bonnie Griffith 32
Border Crossings 12, 13, 47, 48
Botica Agundis 103
bottled water 63
Bovedas Bar 111
Bridge players 8
bridge players 29
Bridge Studio, The 29
Britt Zaist 31
Buddhist oriented meditation 123
Building Permits 136
Burials 108
bus terminal 157
Business Cards 113

C

C. Dewayne Youts 79
Cable TV 52
cable modem 52
Cable TV Service 51
Café de la Parroquia 144
Café etc. 57
Cafe Santa Ana 30

Cancer Support Group 147
Candelaria 44, 65
Candelaria Racquet Club 152
Caracol 40
Carey's 62
Carlos Ramirez Galvan 66
Carmela 117
CASA 70
Casa & Campo 80
Casa Canal 79
Casa Cohen 80
Casa Colon 145
Casa de Cambio 22
Casa de la Cultura 92
Casa de Liza 71
Casa de Papel 27
Casa de Sierra Nevada 109, 115
Casa Diana 78
Casa Don Quixote 145
Casa Hogar Don Bosco 161
Casa Luna Bed & Breakfast 71
Casa Payo 109
Casa Roberto 81
Casas Colonials 78
caterer 146
Cell phones 49
cellulite treatments 116
CENAVI 70
Central Bus Station 156
Centro Bilingual of San Miguel 89, 93
Centro Cultural Ignacio Ramirez 34
Centro de Crecimiento 162
Centro Mexicano de Lengua y Cultura 89
ceramic pots 66
Ceramic Tile 77
Ceramics 33
chairs 79
chandeliers 79
Charcoal and Pencil 32
Charles Miller 56
Charlotte Peltz 121
Chef Maria 34
children's theater 92
chocolate 146
Chorro 40
Christina 120
Christopher Finkelstein 69
Cinema Gemelos 111
Cinemateca 111
Classic yoga 123

Clemente Carbajo 134
Clinica La Joya 101
Club 27 67
Colegio Fray Pedro de Gante 90
colonias 39
comida 145
compraventa 132
Computer Center 35
computer paper 113
computers 55
Computers 101 56
contractor 131, 136
controlled substances 12, 102
Cooking Classes 33
Costco 11
County Institute of Information Access 69
Coyote Canyon Adventures 91
Cremation 108
crutches 108
Curves 124
CyberMacs 56

D

dance floor 111
Daniel Guerra 52, 55
Daniel Guerray 49
Dark Place 91
darkroom techniques 35
David Bar-Chai 34, 93
David Mallory 32
dental surgeon 102
dentist 102
Deportes Aces 152
Dermatology 101
Destinos 150
Digital Camera Club 36
Dining out 143
DISH Network 52
dishes 80
Dog and Puppy Training 121
dog trainer 120
Dolores Hernandez 81
Don Sholl 79
Dr. Alberto Salazar, DDS 102
Dr. Arturo Barrera 100
Dr. Blanca Farias 101
Dr. Carlos Berrera 101
Dr. Cesar Gil Hoyos 105
Dr. Chris Ramaglia 100
Dr. Conchita Garcia Escobedo 105
Dr. Edgardo Vazquez Olmos MVZ 120

Dr. Elvira Cecelia Berrospe 102
Dr. Garcia Glez 105
Dr. Guadalupe Tejada Gomez 102
Dr. Hugo Rosas 100
Dr. Jesus Herrera 102
Dr. Jorge A Martiniez 100
Dr. Jorge Alvarez 100
Dr. Jorge de la Fuente 101
Dr. Juan Bosco Ruiz-Padilla 101
Dr. Laura Elias Urdapileta 102
Dr. Lilian Hernandez 101
Dr. Manuel Velazquez 101
Dr. Robert Merrill Marquez 120
Dr. Salvador Quiroz 100
Dr. Sandra Ramirez 100
Dr. Silvia Azcarate 100, 107
drama coach 31
Drawing and Painting 32
driving range 151
Drs. Francisco Velazquez and Patricia Sobrevilla 101
Druggists 102
dry cleaners 96
dry cleaning 95
Duplicate Bridge Club 29

E

Ebodio Ruiz 76
Eduardo Iglesias 134
El Bacha 144
El Buen Café 144
El Colibri 27
El Grito 110
El Maple 61
El Market Bistro 109
El Nuevo Mundo 78
El Quinto Sol dia Spa 115
El Recreo 92
El Ring 110
El Tomate 62
Electricians, Plumbers and Handymen 76
electronic deposits 12
electronic repairs 55
Elizabeth Noel 78
employment disputes 75
En Agua 68, 110
En Forma Aerobics Studio 124
English-speaking Police Officer 70
ENT 101
entrepreneurship 10
escrow 134

Escrow insurance 133
Escuela de Arte Canek 92
Espino's 62
Estela de Lucia 139
ETN 157
Eva Hunter 36
Evaresto Garcia Jimenez 140
Evo's 80
Express Laundry 95
exercise machines 124
eyeglass repairs 103

F

Fabienne Gauthier 123
Fabrics 78
fabrics 78
facial rejuvenation 116
facial treatments 115
facials 116
Farmacia Guadalajara 103
Farmacia ISSEG 103
Farmapronto 25
Feed the Hungry 162
Feldenkrais Method 125
Ferre, Art 79
Ferreteria Don Pedro 73
Finnegans Pub, Restaurant 109
Fire Department 59
firewood 74
Flamenco 110
Flecha Amarilla 157
Floriade 65
FM-2 86
FM-3 84
FM-T 83
Furniture 78
furniture 78

G

Game Cube 91
garbage collection 26
Gary Berkowitz 36
Gary Burkowitz 33
gas heaters 73
Gas suppliers 26
gays 67
general contractor 139
general medicine 100
Gerardo Lopez Salas 139
Gigante 61
Glass Table Tops 80
Goiricelaya Garcia 134

Goodrich tires 20
Goodyear tires 20
Grace's Sofas 78
Green Angel 59
grooming 120
Guadalupe 41
Guadiana 40
Guillermo Sanchez 105
Guitar 34

H

Hacienda Los Laureles 144
haciendas 159
hair styling 116
hair stylist 116
hair treatments 115
haircuts 117
handicapped child 107
handicapped children 162
Harry's Market 146
health and beauty 115
Health and beauty center 115
health care 99
health insurers 103
Heating 73
Helen Coffee 32
Herberto Guerera 55
Herradura de Plata 157
Historic Walking Tour 158
home care nurses 107
Home Depot 11
Home furnishings 77
home healthcare 107
home insurance 135
homeopathic remedies 105
Homeopaths 105
Horses 121
Hospital Civil 59, 99
Hospital de la Fe 59, 64, 99
Hotel d' Minas 151
Hotel El Santuario Spa & Golf 151
Hotel Posada de la Aldea 91, 152
Hotel Sautto 143
House & Garden Tour 158
Housewares and Decorative Items 80
hypnotherapy 116

I

ID cards 70
Ignacio Ramirez 43

impaired adult 107
Imprenta Martinez 113
IMSS 104
in-home care products 108
Independencia 42
ink cartridges 113
Instituto Allende 31, 125, 150
Instituto de Habla Hispana 150
Instituto de Las Casas 90
insurance appraisals 134
Intercam 23
Interior Design 81
international and domestic flights 158
Internet cafes 57
Internet communications 57
Internet connection 52
Internet connections 47
Internet purchases 47
investment planning 153
Italian seafood 143
Ivan Schuster 64
Izquinapan 43

J

Jack Nicklaus Golf Course 151
Jason Tudisco 56
Javier Garay Lopez 139
Jewelry 33
Jim Bolen 81
Jo Brenzo 35, 36
Joan Elena Goldberg 33, 93
Joan Nagle 125
joint replacements 124
Jose Marin 116
Jose Vasconcelos 88
Josefina R. de Angel 153
Joyous Day Spa 116
Juan Macias 139
Juana Ceballos Gonzalez 116
JuARde 166

K

Keith Keller 32
kennels 120
Kris Rudolph 33, 146

L

La Buena Vida 61, 146
La Carpa 110
La Cava 145
La Cieneguita 45

172.

La Colmena 61
La Conexion 12, 13, 47, 48
La Cucaracha 67, 110
La Europea 145
La Grotta 144
La Lejona 43
La Mansion del Bosque 71
La Muneca 80
La Palapa 144
La Pila 95
La Victoriana 105
La Vida 109
Lalo 76
lamps 79
Land-line Telephones 48
Larry Gassler 56
Las Labrodores 45
Las Puertas 151
Las Terrazas San Miguel 72
Late night scene 110
late night venue 110
Laundries 95
lawyers 134
Le Petit Bar 68
learning Spanish 88
legally rent your property 141
Libros el Tecolote 27
Lighting Fixtures and Ceiling Fans 81
Lilia Trapaga 150
Limerick Pub 67, 109
Linda Cooper 124
Linda Sorin 106
linens 80
L'Invito 143
Lions Club International 147
liquidation 75
Lisa Simms 33, 93
live jazz 143
Lloyds 22
Lloyd's peso accounts 21
local engineer 139
Long Distance 50
Lori Wilson 105
Los Balcones 41
Los Charcos 44
Los Charcos Waldorf Kinder and Primary School 89
Los Frailes 43
Luba 81
Lydia Wong 123

M

Magnolia 78
Malanquin 43
Malanquin Country Club 90, 151, 152
Mama Mia 110, 143
Mama Mia's 109
manicures 115, 116
ManRey Silva 66
Margarito Galvan 77
Martha Hernandez 116
Martha Lieberman 55
massage 115
massages 116
masseuse 116
MDT Computadoras 113
mechanics 19
Medical Air Services Association 99
Medical Emergencies 59
meditation 123
Meditation Center 123
Meditation Center of San Miguel 123
Melanie Nance 153
Memoirs 37
Mexicam culture 5
Mexican Advisor 153
Mexican drivers license 17
Mexican insurance 15
Mexican license plate 16
Mexican music 146
Mexican residency 83
Mexican Wills 133
Mexico Advisor 134
Mexpro 104
Meynarda Morales 93
Michele Vallon 146
Michelin tires 20
microcurrent facials 116
microderm abrasion 116
Microdyn 62
Ministerio Publico 70
MITU 80
Monarca 64
Monex 23
Montecillo Ranch 122
mortgages 130, 131
Mosqueta 77
motor scooter rental 152
movies 111
Mujeres Productoras 162

Multicom 51
Municipal Institute of Women 70
Music and Dance 34

N

Neighborhoods 39
Netflix.com 113
Nicole Bisgaard 139
Night Kitchen Caterers's 146
Nina Wisniewski 32
Nirvana Restaurant-Fusion 143
Notaries 132
notario publico 132
nternet and E-mail Connections 52
Nurseries 65
Nutri Verdi 145

O

ob-gyn 100
Obraje 41
Office Depot 12
Office Max 12
office supplies 113
Ojo de Agua 40
Olimpia Miranda 120
Olimpo 42
Omnibus de Mexico 158
Opthalmology 101
Optica Allende 103
Optica San Miguel 103
optometrists 103
orphanage 161
orthopedic equipment 108
orthopedic shoes 108
Ortopedia J. Ortiz 108
Our Caring Community 107
Outdoor Furniture 79

P

Packet8 50
paella 110
Painting with Ink and Watercolors 31
Pancho and Lefty's 67
Pancho Segura 120
Papeleria Heros Insurgentes 113
Papier Mache 33
papier mache 93
Parador de Cortijo 44
Paris 96
parking lots 20

patio furniture 80
Patio sets 79
Patricia Merrill Marguez 139
Patronato Pro Ninos 158
Patsy DuBois 34
pedicures 115, 116
Pegasso Plus 157
Permaculture Community 45
perscription drugs 12
personal trainer 124
peso bank accounts 21
pet adoption 162
pets for adoption 121
photo transfer and manipulation 35
Photography and Digital Camera Club 35
Photoshop Techniques 35
physical therapy 162
Pilates 124
pillows 78
Plastic surgery 101
Play Station II 91
PMC (Promotion of Mexican Culture) 159
Poder Notarial 133
Police 59
por favor 2
Power of Attorney 133
Premium Home Health Care Providers 107
Primera Plus 157
Printmaking 33
private parties 146
private schools 87, 88
Property managers 140
Public buses 156
Public school 87
Punto G 57

Q

Qigong 125

R

Radio Shack 108
Ramon Gonzalez 79
ranches 159
Rancho La Loma 122
Raoul Rodriguez 153
Rebecca Peterson 32, 92
Receiving and Sending Mail 47
Red Cross Ambulance 59

Reflex Center, The 116
reflexologist 106
Reflexology 116
rehabilitation programs 124
reinvention 8
Rent a Car 20
rental 111
rental DVDs 111
renting 127
Residencial La Luz 43
Restaurant Lila 145
restaurants 143
Reyes Retana 134
Rhea's Massage 116
Richard Crissman 37
Rincon Espanol 110
Ritchie Granados 155
Robert de Gast 35
Rodriguez/Navarro 33
Rotary Club 147

S

Sally Riewald 37
Salon and Spa de Robert 116
Salvador Soto 134
San Antonio 40
San Felipe 42
San Juan de Dios 41
San Miguel Health and Fitness Center 124
San Miguel Travel 159
San Rafael 42
Santa Julia 42
Santo Domingo Sports Club 91, 124
Santuario Hogar Guadalupano Mexiquito 161
Sarah Berges 57
satellite connections 52
Saturday Adventure Tours 159
sauna 115
Sazon 34, 80
Seamstress 81
Sears 12
seat cushions 78
senior citizen care 163
Sensual Chocolatiers 146
Sergio Hernandez 153
service to the Mexico City airport 155
Shaklee 116
Shari Reynolds 56
Short-term boarding 120

shuttle service to Leon 155
Skidmore Smith 35
Sky 52
Skype 50
Sociedad Protectora de Animales 162
soil 65
Sol Y Luna 152
Solutions 12, 13
Sonke Stuck 52
SPA 162
Spanish 149
Spanish language classes 149
Spanish summer day camp 93
Spanish Through Cinema 150
spinal problems 124
Sra. Gabriela Nieto 82
St. Michael's Canine Center 120
St. Paul's Church 108
stationery 113
steaks 109, 143
Sue Bolli 55
Sue Lawrence 124
summer riding 91
Sweat Your Prayers 125
swimming program 91

T

tables 79
Taboada 44
Taboada Hot Springs 125
Tai Chi 123
Tai Chi Chuan 125
Tapi Centro 82
tax returns 153
Taxis 156
Tee Seals 81
TelCel 49
Tele Cable 51, 52
Telephone Repairs 49
TELMEX 48, 49, 50, 53
tennis courts 151, 152
Teocalli 159
The Insider's Guide to San Miguel 165
The Lions Club 159
The Little Clay School 93
The Novel 37
Tilloglobe 104
Tim Wacher 66
Tintoreria Franco Lavanderia 95
Tintorerias del Bajio 96
Tio Lucas 109, 143

Tirado 45
title search 134
Tourist visas 83
Towing 59
trailriding 122
Transportes Del Norte 158
travel agencies 155
Turisticos Rodriguez 155, 156
Twenty-Four Hour Association 108
Twenty-Four Hour Care Services 107

U

U.S. MediCare 103
Unisono net 53
University training 88
Upholstery and Slip Covers 82
urniture maker 79
utility bills 25

V

Valerie Jennings 56
vegetarian restaurant 145
Verizon 51
vet 120
Veterinarians 120
Viajes de San Miguel 155, 158
Viajes Vertiz 158
Victoria Challancin 34
Victoria Robbins 89
Vidiios y Cristales de San Miguel 80
Villa Jacaranda 29, 111
Villa Scorpio 72
visas 83
Vivero Primavera 65
Vonage 50

W

Walking Mexico's Colonial Heartland 166
Walmart 12
Walter Weber's 151
water aerobics 125
water company 26
Water Purification 63
water wonderland 92
Web pages 56
Wednesday Lunch Group 9
Wellness for Life 115
William J. Conaway 166

Women in Change 161
Workshop for Pros 36
world cuisines 144
wrought iron furniture 79

X

X Boxes 91
XOTE 92

Y

Yoga by Norman 123
Yoga classes 123

Z